# SELL A MILLION!

## 101 Tips for Furniture & Mattress Store Owners to Sell Another Million Dollars or More This Year

## Pete Primeau

# Table of Contents

# Foreword

Pete Primeau has discovered the secret to success. It's a para-dox. By putting others needs before one's own, produces more success than having success as one's goal. This book has the goal of making anyone that takes the time to read it more successful. But it requires more than just reading. One must put these great tips into practice. The good news it. It's easy to do. Keep this excellent book at your store and pick out a new tip, learn it, use it, make it a part of your selling process and then go to another. In short order, you will improve.

Pete is a wonderful guy and is a seasoned veteran in the home furnishings industry. Old school reps, such as Pete had to know, apply and teach most every aspect of the home furnishings and mattress business, from marketing, merchandising, inventory control to advertising and sales training. That's why this book is so valuable. It contains years of knowledge and wisdom that Pete has acquired though his experiences. I highly recommend it to any and everyone in the retail mattress and furniture industry.

Gerry Morris


Gerry Morris is an author, consultant and training coach with more than 20 years of experience in the mattress industry. Morris' Inner Spring training company has a strategic partnership with The Furniture Training Co. to offer a premium online training course, "Sell More Mattresses with Gerry Morris." To view the course, visit-www.furnituretrainingcompany.com.

"Take the word mattress and furniture out of this book and insert any other industry and this book is still gold. Home Furnishings is blessed to have a man like Pete who cares so deeply about his faith, his family, his customers and his industry. This book is packed with actionable (boots on the ground) wisdom that work in the real world. You won't find theory here. Pete does a fantastic job of equipping the reader with meaningful information that will drive business.

"Steven Covey said, 'To know and not to do is really not to know.' I believe there will be two types of people who read this book. People who think they already know and will not act and people who take these words and apply them to their business forever changing their future in a powerful way."

Doug Stewart
http://about.me/Doug_Stewart


"What Pete Primeau has assembled for mattress and furniture stores with this book is much more than just 101 tips. Each idea in this book builds on the one before it, providing you with a complete marketing and sales machine.

"This book is not purely theoretical; the vast majority of the 101 ideas have been put into action by Pete himself. The ideas he hasn't implemented in his own businesses over the years, he's seen work for other businesses. There is no fluff in this book.

"If you want to grow your sleep or furniture store, there's no better place to start than this book. Learn from Pete's experience and advice and then go and implement. You'll see your sales grow, your customers will love you - and just maybe your hair will grow back too!"

Simon Aronowitz
http://www.thetestimonialguru.com

# Introduction

I started in the furniture business in 1982. My first mentor was George Cooley who taught me how to be an RSA, a sales manager, and a rep. I learned how to master the art of the sale at retail from Angel Guiterez. Unfortunately Angel passed much too young. Thank You to my former boss Larry Koreness, who believed in me more than I believed in myself. Larry challenged me, goaded me, and coached me to become more than I was before him. I will never forget him. I probably would never would have become a rep if it wasn't for the kindness and the coaching of Nat Bernstein.

I have been blessed to meet, work with, and learn from some truly great retailers. There hasn't been a dealer or a salesperson that I haven't learned from.

Several years ago Simon Aronowitz, my testimonial guy, introduced me to Jeff Glagnocavo, an award winning marketer and veteran of the mattress industry at a marketing conference. I was not familiar with Jeff's store in Lancaster, PA or with his business systems.

I learned very quickly that Jeff and his business partner, Ben McClure, were special. Not only are they pioneers offering retailers a better way to retail, but they are two of the most honest men I have ever met. I am proud to call them friends!

I could not have written this book without Jeff and his ideas which I feel are the best in the industry. I am a customer of Ben & Jeff's, as I hope you will become one also. To be completely transparent, Jeff & Ben are customers of mine as well. I've included Jeff's information throughout this book and if you buy

Jeff's products or services you should know that I might receive a pat on the back, a free dinner or even a check. You should also know that all my customers receive Jeff & Ben's lowest prices.

I hope this book gives you new ideas that you will prosper from. Please read it and then read it again and then implement the ideas into your business! Please call me with any questions that you may have. I am here to help you grow your business!

Also be sure to subscribe to my "No BS Sales Marketing & More Podcast For Furniture & Mattress Stores" as I will be from time to time taking a chapter and discussing it in depth as to exactly how you can implement the recommendation in your business. You can access this link (and all the other web links) from this page: http://www.peteprimeau.com/book-links.

I also run a fun, and informative Facebook group called the **No BS Sales School For Furniture & Mattress Sales People**. You can access it from here:

http://www.peteprimeau.com/book-links.

Sell A Million!

Pete Primeau

PS - As you read this book, read with an open mind and be receptive to the unique and proven tips contained within these pages and please remember - Your Business IS NOT Different!

PPS - This book is meant to be highlighted, dog eared, sentences circled and you may even tear pages out! When you wear out your first copy I'll happily give you another one.

# 1. I'm Not?

I have a shocking truth to start this book off with.

*You're not in the business you think you're in!*

You may think you're a retail store owner.

But you aren't!

**You are in the "*marketing of*" a retail store business.**

*See the difference?*

It's vital to understand and remember your #1 job as a business owner is the marketing of your business, because without effective marketing, which converts into sales, NOTHING ELSE MATTERS!

This may make you feel a bit uncomfortable, especially if you're not marketing-oriented at this point in time (I will attempt to change that shortly), but it's important for you to keep an open mind and understand how vitally important marketing is to you, your family and your employees. The rest of this book is dedicated to helping you get better at marketing with 100 more "*high impact*" marketing tips, strategies and ideas. Profit from them!

"THEY'RE STICKY NOTES
WITH MY SPECIAL OFFER."

# 2. Always Be Marketing!

For the success-oriented business owner, there's never a day off when it comes to the marketing of their business. As a matter of fact, as I mentioned in the previous chapter, you're really not in the business you think you're in. In reality, you're in the marketing business – every day. This is true whether you like it or not.

So for example, a carpet cleaner is really not in the carpet cleaning business. She's in the marketing of a carpet cleaning business and in order to rise above the competition and succeed, she must never forget this truth and she must *"Always Be Marketing!"*.

I like to instruct business owners to keep their marketing radar on 24 hours a day, 7 days a week and look for opportunities to communicate more effectively with your prospects and customers. Always be asking yourself questions like,

*What's happening in the news or current events which I can leverage in my marketing?*

*Is there a special holiday or event coming up which allows me to create a unique marketing message?*

When you're in A.B.M. mode, you'll see opportunities all around you (that you probably didn't see before), which will allow you to offer greater value to your customers and prospects. Look for inspiration everywhere. Do look outside of our industry for ideas constantly.

# 3. Always Ask for and Give Multiple Ways for Response

I'm a huge fan of direct response marketing, which is often a different style of marketing then you're familiar with, or may have studied in school or seen on TV or print.

The fundamental principle behind direct response marketing is to always give the recipient a reason to respond now. No marketing message ever goes out with some reason to respond in some type of fashion within a specific time-frame.

If you don't ask for a response... 9 times out of 10, the person you're marketing too will simply ignore you.

In every marketing effort you create, give the recipient a good (or better yet, several good) reasons why they should take immediate action. Then make sure you offer them different ways to respond. Here are a few typical marketing response channels:

- Telephone
- Mail
- Email
- Web site

- Fax
- Text
- Social Media
- In-person

Remember, always ask for a response and give simple ways to respond. By simply doing this, your marketing will improve and your results will improve.

# 4. Always Follow-Up!

You know how in real estate shopping, everyone says the three most important things you need are location, location and location? Well, I say in business, the three most important things are follow-up, follow-up, and more follow-up! *Why?* Very few sales are ever made with just one contact. For years, the closing percentage on mattresses has been just under 30%. The closing percentage for furniture is well under 20%. For example, an average business owner will run an ad and when somebody responds to that ad, if they don't buy immediately, they stop marketing to that person. They let a potential customer who they just spent a whole bunch of money advertising to, walk out the door without any additional follow-up!

Remember, few sales are made on the first try. It typically takes 3-7 contacts to convert a prospect into a paying customer, and the higher the dollar transaction, the more contacts are required. So after spending money to market to prospects to get their attention, make sure you have a method and a system to capture their information for follow-up marketing, and don't forget the after sale follow-up! When I worked at Kronheim's Furniture, we had a drawing for a Free Vacation Trip twice a year. I would have them fill it out and write my name on the back and put it in the box. I would then send a follow-up Thank You note to the customer. A few times over the nine years I sold, retail customers came in to buy from me after canceling a sale with one of my competitors because of my follow-up.

You can differentiate your business by simply sending a thank you note or some other form of follow-up after the sale. If you already do this, pat yourself on the back and then add more steps to your follow-up. It will pay huge dividends. I promise.

"DID I GET HERE IN TIME?"

# 5. Always Have a Deadline!

*"An offer without a deadline is not an offer."*

Good, effective marketing is made up of several fundamental components. We've already seen a few and throughout the rest of this book, I will share several more.

Always having a deadline in your marketing offers is one of those fundamentals you must always keep in mind. In today's crazy-busy world, everybody is too distracted to notice your marketing and you must do what you can to get them to take action now! Deadlines help accomplish this, which is why you always want to have a deadline when you make an offer. Here are a few deadline ideas to consider:

- Always have a specific deadline date and let people know what happens after this date.

- Have a deadline for parts of your offer and/or specified bonuses and/or discounts.

- Create *"act now pricing"* which offers a discount and where prices go up on a certain dates. This is common in event marketing.

- Offer bonuses for the *"first x-number of buyers."*

- Create real, limited quantities.

- Create *"fear of loss by delay"* in your offer, such as: *"Every day you wait to buy a new mattress, your sore back will remind you."*

"THEY'RE BETTER THAN COMMENT CARDS."

# 6. Help Them Testify!

Social proof that reaffirms your product or service does what you say it will do, is mandatory these days. Just about everybody does some sort of research before they visit a restaurant for the first time, hire an electrician or buy a car. This is why sites like Angie's List™, Amazon Reviews and Google+ are so popular these days. Create a system to ask for and use testimonials and reviews in your business. Typically the best time to do this is when the customer is happiest (at the time of purchase, delivery, etc.). Here are a few ideas to get you started:

- Create a short customer survey and have all customers fill out. Ask for a testimonial

- Hand out a flyer during the sales process asking them to give you a positive review online.

- Take a picture with your customer at the time of sale or when they receive their delivery.

- Use social media to give online fans a way to leave their comments.

Collect these testimonials and use them in all your marketing – offline and online. Create a testimonial book and leave copies around your office or store. The effort you put into this will come back to you exponentially. If for some reason the consumer is unwilling to give your business a positive testimonial or review, that is a warning to you that some type of intervention is needed. Be willing to change a process or even an employee if you are consistently uncovering the same complaint. Businesses, like people, are always changing for better or for worse - they do not stay the same. So commit to changing your business for the better.

"I AM SO GLAD YOU TOLD ME
ABOUT THIS PLACE!"

# 7. Earn Referrals

*"Do what you do so well – and so uniquely – that people cannot resist telling others about you."*

~ Walt Disney

Collecting testimonials is important in your marketing efforts. Equally important is asking for referrals from happy and satisfied customers.

Studies have shown one of the *"easiest"* types of sales to make is the referral sale whereby a prospect comes to you based on a reference from an existing customer.

I don't know about you, but I like easy sales.

The strategies for getting referrals is much like the testimonial strategies I outlined. The biggest thing is just getting started and consistently asking for them.

Second, you need a system to ask for and reward referrals.

Create a *"referral culture"* in your business and let your customers know you appreciate (and expect) referrals. Create a rewards program and award prizes. Always recognize customers, who do refer, in your newsletters, emails, in pictures, etc. Done right, a referral system is a sales machine for your business. As importantly recognize and reward your employees who get the most referrals as well.

# 8. Me, Learn?

Direct response marketing has been around for over 100 years and if you study any of the great marketing copywriters and experts during this time, you'll see they are all students of direct response marketing.

Direct response marketing differs from traditional marketing in a number of ways, including the ability to track and measure results. For the business owner, it's a much more effective and efficient way to promote their business. Here are a few important keys to effective direct response marketing:

- Have a crystal-clear picture of who your ideal customer is and craft your marketing around getting this person's attention and response

- Have a specific call-to-action with a deadline

- Follow-up multiple times with multiple media

- Reward immediate action

- Track, measure, analyze, and adjust your marketing

# 9. Got Data?

Did you know one of the greatest assets in your business is your customer database? This is the real value of your business and it should be treated as the gold mine it really is. It needs to be updated on a regular basis and purged once every year or two.

Many business owners neglect or use antiquated methods to maintain their customer database. The days of keeping your customer database on paper in a file cabinet (or even a simple Microsoft Excel file) are long over for the modern day business owner!

All business owners should be using some type of customer relationship management system (CRM) to build and maintain not only a customer database, but also a prospect database. These computer-based systems allow you to quickly and easily create follow-up campaigns, track sales, maintain notes, and much more.

While the pain of setting them up can be real, in the long term, they allow you to do some many important and vital things, you simply cannot be without one.

CRM systems like AWeber™, Infusionsoft™ and others are designed for the business owner looking for automation systems which can help you put much of your marketing an auto-pilot. Automate as much as you can. It will allow you to get more done in less time, freeing you up to do important strategic thinking which is vital to your store's long term financial health.

# 10. Power of a Mastermind

Being an entrepreneur and business owner can be a lonely experience at times, especially when it comes to developing and evaluating new marketing ideas and promotions. This why few successful business owners are *"doing it on their own"* and instead, have some type of go-to network for bouncing ideas around.

Napoleon Hill coined the *"master mind"* in his Laws of Success which he wrote in the 1920's and it's still applicable to you today. The coming together of like-minded individuals for a common purpose can result in amazing things, which is why I have been a part of similar groups for years.

You can do the same thing by creating a group of local, success-oriented business owners and meeting once a month. You can also ask several key customers to be a part of an ongoing customer advisory panel to help you flesh out appropriate marketing promotions.

Try it and see for yourself how the power of the *"master mind"* can result in amazing things! My dinners at the furniture markets are actually the beginning of a mastermind. I bring dealers from non-competing geographies and marketing experts together for dinner at High Point Market usually at Fleming's in Greensboro, NC. We share success stories and we share resources to help my dealers make more money. Everyone likes a great meal, but learning how to make more money from a fellow store owner is something my dealers love!

At our last dinner. fellow mattress store owner and market-er extraordinaire Jeff Giagnocavo, and The Testimonial Guru,

Simon Aronowitz ,shared so many great ideas with my dealers that I thought their heads were going to pop! It was fun and educational at the same time. My good friend and co-host of The No BS Sales, Marketing & More Podcast For Furniture & Mattress Stores, Doug Stewart, was like a kid in a candy store. We all had fun learning from each other that night. Dealers shared resources with each other that reduced their costs and made them more money. One dealer had a printer who prints good quality flyers for much less than anyone at the table had ever heard of. Another dealer had a great resource for financing. I was really proud of my dealers when they swapped phone numbers and promised to stay in touch with each other. When it was time to leave, I could tell no one wanted to leave. It was a great experience for all.

Masterminding with other furniture and mattress stores owners is a great way to grow your knowledge quickly. In a properly structured mastermind, there are serious accountability mechanisms put into place. This helps you get done what you commit to. The fastest way to success is through a well run mastermind.

# 11. Define Your Ideal Target

Having a crystal-clear picture of your ideal target market is critically important when developing marketing campaigns and promotions that get results.

Let me clarify this with a more practical example. I love to fish and I like to go fishing for many different types of fish.

Each type of fish and environment requires me to use a specific type of fishing rod and bait. A small rod and worm will not work when trying to attract a large catfish or walleye. Since I know what I am going after, I know what to use.

Good effective marketing is no different. I need to know who I'm trying to attract before I can start, so I can use the right offer (the bait) and the right media (the rod) to find them and land them as a customer.

Invest in the time to analyze your best customer and the people you like doing business with. Create a profile of this person (income level, education, where they live, what they do, etc.) and develop marketing campaigns and strategies to find more of them. Your customer profile will change over time for a variety of reasons. The great retailers change their marketing, merchandising, display, sales training as well as their policies and procedures to be in sync with their consumer base. They do not change because of opinions or guess work. They change because of data that they constantly collect and analyze.

# 12. Wake Customers Up!

Weak, wimpy ordinary offers cannot be expected to produce exceptional results – the kind you are looking for.

In today's age of ultra-competition, it's simply unreasonable to believe boring and typical offers will get attention and response.

Yet most marketers put forward mundane offers day in and day out and then grumble about the disappointing results. Remember the six hour sales from the eighties? Do you remember the treasure chest sales from the nineties? By the way, with a new spin both could work today.

Whether you are creating a lead-generation offer, product or service offer, sales offer – whatever – you must do the hard work of thinking up something that stands out and gets noticed and makes the person receiving it say, *"I'd be a fool if I said no to this."*

Think about your own experiences...what has motivated you in the past? What has gotten you to say *"yes"* and take immediate action?

Think outside-the-box and craft offers which rise above all the typical ones out there and gets your target market to take action.

# 13. Create a Unique Value Proposition

A person who has never done business with you walks up and asks, "*Why should I choose your business versus any other competitive option available to me including doing nothing at all?*" Does this question leave you tongue-tied, or can you quickly and persuasively give an answer? If you can't, you are probably in trouble or soon will be.

Your response indicates whether or not you have performed one of the most fundamental and important steps in marketing your business: the development of a unique value proposition, or UVP. In today's market, it's critical that you differentiate yourself from your competition. An effective UVP is short, memorable, and meaningful. Your UVP is about commitments and promises. It should reflect your passion and energy for serving your customers. Ask yourself:

*"What is our company committed to providing to our customers or clients that nobody else can?"*

Your UVP is not about your financial goals or product/ service features. Your UVP is about meeting your customers' or clients' needs and it should be the focal point around which all of your marketing messages are built. Coming up with a clear and unique UVP doesn't cost you money, but it does require careful thought and consideration. You may start this process by writing out on paper what great and unique experiences that you can provide that other competitors are not.

After that step is complete, start by asking yourself is this doable? Are the steps necessary to deliver this ideal service practical? It might be challenging to live up to this new ideal consumer experience but it can pay huge dividends. This might sound crazy, but it should not be easy to deliver. It should be difficult. If it's not, your competitors will copy you if they can figure it out.

Here is the most important question after the UVP is established: "Can we consistently deliver this?" If yes, then do everything in your power to deliver it. Remember automation is your friend - the more of it that can be automated, the better. Here is mine: I am a wholesale rep so mine and yours will be different. Get creative and have fun with your UVP.

*We do the right thing all the time even when it costs us money.*

*Everyone says it - We Live It! Ask me how!*

# 14. Evaluate and Monitor Your Advertising Campaigns

Marketing is not a *"set it and forget it"* component of business. The value of direct response marketing is that it allows you to know if people are responding to your campaigns and to adjust it as needed.

My suggestion is to hold weekly or at least bi-weekly marketing meetings with your staff and review all your numbers. If you run a one-person business, take time each week to generate and review the numbers.

Are people responding to your lead generation offers? Are customers buying upsells? Are customers coming back for repeat purchases? Are your customers giving your store 5 star online consumer reviews? Are they gladly giving you positive testimonials? Are they giving you referrals?

The average business owner spends little, if any time, evaluating the effectiveness of their marketing and then more importantly adjusting them where necessary.

If your marketing is not producing the kinds of numbers you think it should, invest the time to objectively look at everything you're doing and make adjustments, try something new, change things up. Do not neglect this. The overall health and vibrancy of your business depends on you making little improvements all the time.

# 15. Handle It!

It's been said, *"Nothing is more powerful than goodwill, except ill will."*

As realistic business owners we know we cannot make 100% of our customers happy 100% of the time, but it doesn't mean that we don't try.

If you have a dissatisfied customer, make it right – fast or sooner.

In today's day and age of ultra-connectedness, it only takes one upset consumer to post something on a web site or social media that could potentially damage your brand and cause others to pause before doing business with you.

*"Reputation management"* is becoming an important issue for all business owners and is something to be aware of every day.

Consider creating a customer hotline or special email for customers to use to provide feedback and make sure employees know how to handle complaints in a professional and courteous manner. Empower your employees to make it right. Customer service cannot and will not wait in this new world of instant gratification.

# 16. Have Your Marketing Radar Always On!

I mentioned your *"marketing radar"* in a previous chapter, but I think this concept is so important, I want to go into more detail about this easy-to-do strategy.

Smart marketers are always on the lookout for current events, news, examples, people, etc. which offer an opportunity to build a marketing message around.

In our media-driven society, creating a marketing message, sales promotion or event around something going on in the news is a sure way to get attention and response.

But unless you are constantly open and receptive to looking for these types of opportunities, you'll miss them like 99% of store owners do.

A simple strategy to use is to always have a way to jot down impromptu notes, whether it's a simple paper tablet or a digital device. As you see and think of opportunities, write them down and then make sure to take advantage of them before the opportunity passes. I have forgotten some great ideas in my life , please don't miss the next great idea for your business. I keep paper and pen next to my bed so if I wake up in the middle of the night I can capture it!

# 17. What's In It For Them!

Do you know the #1 radio station in the world, listened to by every prospect and customer?

It's WII-FM.

WII-FM stands for *"what's in it for me?"* which is the main question your prospects and customers are constantly asking themselves when considering your product or service.

At their most basic core, they really don't care about you or your business. They only care about what your product/service/ business is going to do for them and all smart marketers must remind themselves of this fundamental truth and never lose sight of it.

This means when you create a marketing promotion, newspaper ad, email, whatever, you're constantly approaching the task at hand, NOT from your needs and wants, but from the needs and wants of your recipient. Always answer the question, *"What's in it for me?"*

Tune into WII-FM and profit. The better you are at walking in your customer's shoes and asking the same questions they ask both spoken and unspoken the more perfectly targeted your marketing will be!

"AS MUCH AS I APPRECIATE YOUR
ENTHUSIASM, THIS ISN'T EXACTLY THE
'TARGET YOUR CUSTOMER' MARKETING
PLAN I HAD IN MIND."

# 18. Know Your Who

Successful marketers know before they can even think about creating a marketing piece or campaign, they have to invest the time and energy into creating a crystal-clear picture of the person they're marketing to.

Do you take the time and effort to think about your *"who"* before you map out your campaign?

Most marketers and business owners DON'T invest the time to think about their who before they begin their marketing and the result is marketing that doesn't reach its potential.

In the previous chapter, I showed you the power of answer the question *"what's in it for me?"* and until you know exactly who you are trying to market to, you cannot answer this question.

Before you start your next marketing effort, take some time and create a profile of the person who you want to respond. *Where do they live? Are they married? Retired? Have kids in school? What are their hopes? What are their fears?*

The more questions you can ask and answer and then use the answers in your marketing, the more effective your next campaign will be.

# 19. Clean Sells!

If you have a retail store it's imperative to keep it as clean and sanitary as possible. My good friend and dealer Jim Hick's from Mattress Mart in Zanesville, Ohio is fanatical about this. When he shops competitors he looks at the store through the eyes of the consumer. Often when he looks up when he is laying down on a bed he is amazed at what he sees. This attention to detail keeps Jim's store profitable year after year even in down economies.

Depending on your target market, this could have a huge impact on repeat business. Your customers have more and more choices to buy their furniture and mattresses from. Offering a pleasing and clean environment to shop in could possibly turn the balance in your favor.

Today, customers notice everything (even when you don't think they notice) and guess what? Few will say anything to you, but they will let you know by never visiting again or telling their friends.

- Filthy bathrooms?
- Bad odors?
- Cobwebs in the corners?
- Burned out light bulbs?
- Stained floors?

Not acceptable if you want to run a successful business and you must make it a priority to keep your place of business clean and inviting as possible. Promote somebody to C.C.O. (Chief Cleanliness Officer) and make it their job to stay on top of this. I was so frustrated with one of my dealers once that I spent hours cleaning his restroom. To my surprise he kept it clean after that.

# 20. Easy Money

As you already know there is no easy money. But you should make it easy for customers to give you money. I've worked with hundreds of stores over the years. Many stores make it hard for customers to give them money.

Making it easy for customer to give you money means to have as many different ways to get paid as you are comfortable with. I realize not all of these methods are right for every business owner, but take a moment to review this list and see if there are any you can add. If you sell furniture or mattresses on your website PayPal could be important to you.

- Cash and checks
- All major credit cards
- Debit cards
- Electronic payment (e.g. PayPal)
- Multi-payment plans
- Layaway plans
- Online order forms
- Fax back order forms

# 21. Coach Team Members

There's a saying: *"inspect what you expect"* and as business owners we must stay on top of what employees and team members are doing. I wish it was different but it isn't. You could implement every strategy in this book and still fail, if your team is not on board and doing things the way you need them done, especially if they have direct contact with prospects and customers.

I have seen this happen more times than I like to remember, where a store owner has done everything right and an employee undermines the entire system with the wrong attitude, behavior or knowledge. It can kill a business. Don't let it happen to you!

The best way to ensure your team has the same vision and follow through is to make them part of the marketing process and reward them for going extra steps. Hold frequent marketing strategy meetings where everybody has input. Get team members' buy in and agreement with new marketing initiatives and systems. Help them realize their success is directly related to your customers' success.

As the owner, it's ultimately up to you to make sure employees and team members are doing the job you expect them to be doing. Stay on top of this all the time and see the difference it can make in your business. You might need to be patient with some of your employees at the beginning. Once they see and feel your commitment they will come on board. If they don't, after a reasonable amount of time and consistent feedback they might no longer be a fit for your company. Please do not arbitrarily fire people in my name. Only after they don't respond to feedback over time do I suggest the F word!

# 22. Offer a Solid Guarantee
# Part 1

Let's face it... doing business these days is not easy. We're all up against more resistance and skepticism than ever before and we need to make sure every tool in our marketing toolkit is working to its potential.

Your guarantee (either a product or service one) should be one of the foundational components of your marketing and business strategy. If you don't have one - you need one. And if you do have one, this is the perfect time to revisit it to ensure it's doing everything you need it to do.

The whole point of your guarantee is to remove as much perceived risk from the purchase of your product or service as possible. I say "*perceived*" because even if you believe there are absolutely ZERO concerns with your product or service, it doesn't matter because it only matters what your prospect or customer thinks.

By removing as much of the risk as possible, you're letting people know you're a reliable and ethical business owner, who truly has their best interests at heart and will stand by whatever it is you're selling.

# 23. Offer a Solid Guarantee Part 2

To begin the process of creating a strong guarantee, you must absolutely remove yourself (and your beliefs and mental hurdles) from the picture and look at it through the eyes of your prospect.

This is harder than it sounds, since the tendency is to be too conservative as you go through this process. The point is not to *"just have a guarantee."* The point is to have a strong, unique guarantee that drives more sales and order to do this, you're probably going to initially say..."*Ouch this hurts!"*

Often times crafting a strong guarantee makes the business owner cringe and if it doesn't, it's probably not as strong and unique and it could be. It's part of human nature to feel like a strong, customer-oriented guarantee is going to INCREASE the number of people who take you up on it, but more times than not, this is not the case.

Studies have shown, if your product or service does what you say it does, then the increased number of sales, because of the presence of your guarantee, will outweigh the number of people who take you up on your guarantee.

"WOW! YOU MADE THIS JUST FOR ME?"

# 24. Personalize & Profit

The more a person feels as if your marketing, products and services were created specifically for them, the better your results. One effective way to accomplish this is the use of personalized marketing.

With today's computer technology, you can create personalized marketing campaigns quickly and easily that make the recipient feel as if you are talking directly to them and nobody else.

The simplest way to accomplish this is to always ask for and use a person's name when communicating with them (either face to-face, in print or online). We humans like hearing and seeing our name in print and it's a powerful and simple way to get attention. In addition to using a person's name in your marketing, here is a list of other things you can easily personalize:

- Their location
- The # of years they've been a customer
- The last time they visited your business
- The anniversary of their first visit
- The name and details of the product or service purchased
- Their birthday or other special event

# 25. Quantify Value

This one tip could be worth hundreds, if not thousands of dollars to you!

Throughout your marketing (and sales) process it is important that you always quantify the value you've included in the offer and put discrete, realistic values so the person considering knows exactly what it's worth.

For example if you're giving away a free gift to drive prospects into your business, articulate the actual value of the gift in your marketing. Don't just say "R*eceive a free book when you visit*" and instead say "R*eceive a free book, worth $35.00, when you visit.*" Printing a price on a report, book or ebook can help establish value.

Many times, to close a larger-priced sale, a business owner will bundle in valued-added products and services. Make sure you include line item price values for each and add them up so the prospect knows exactly the value of the entire package.

Don't leave the math up to reader.

Help people understand the value of what you're offering by explicitly telling and showing them the value in dollars and cents.

# 26. Eight Marketing Truths

People are funny and we, as business owners, must remember this fundamental truth. Here are a few other "*truths*" to keep in mind as you craft your next marketing promotion.

**People are procrastinators.** Be sure to give them at least one reason to act now.

**People are skeptical.** Make sure your marketing message is believable.

**People are lazy.** Make it easy for them to respond.

**People avoid risk.** Include an iron-clad guarantee to help them feel comfortable.

**People pay little or no attention to things which do not interest them.** Target your marketing!

**People want to know "*what's in it for me?*"** Be sure to tell them clearly and personally.

**People are easily confused.** Make sure your message is crystal clear. Never assume they understand. It is our responsibility to confirm that our customer understands.

**People want to know "*when.*"** Tell them how long fulfillment, delivery or other actions will take (and make sure you meet that commitment). Actually build in a little extra time so that your company under promises and over delivers.

"YES MRS. SMITH. WE HAVE
SOMETHING FOR LITTLE JOHNNY,
STUART AND MEGAN."

# 27. Segment Your Database

Maintaining a usable marketing database of prospects, current customer and past customers is very smart and is a huge, valuable asset for your business.

One of the smartest things you can do with this database is to segment it or *"slice and dice it"* so you can send specific and targeted messages to *"sub lists."* Let me explain with an example.

Let's say you have 1,000 prospects in your database which have full contact information (e.g. name, mailing address and email address). For this example, this is your *"full list."* You could then create sub lists from this complete list based on the towns each person lives in and send out a sales letter or email with the headline *"Special Sale for People Who Live in XYZ Town."* Follow-up marketing would stress the same targeted message.

This simple, yet effective use of a targeted message will increase response, since the person receiving says, *"Hey this is for me!"* The only efficient way to do this type of targeted marketing is by segmenting your database and sending specific marketing to specific people. This advanced strategy could add thousands of dollars of extra sales every year. More importantly the more targeted your marketing is the better the relationship will be with the consumer. Which leads to better testimonials and more referrals.

Your list must be segmented by product categories as well as up-sale offers. If someone buys a mattress and protector but not sheets, frames, and pillows separate marketing campaigns can be developed to maximize the value of each customer. Did they buy a bedroom but no nightstands? If they move to a bigger house do you think they would appreciate an offer to buy night stands before their group is discontinued? Of course they would.

When I worked at Kronheim's Furniture we advertised and offered many children's correlate bedroom sets. Today this information would be in our customer database. Back then I kept all my customer's information on 3x5 index cards. At one of our sales meetings we found out one of those bedrooms were discontinued. I ran back to the store, sorted my index cards, called all my customers and helped my customers buy thousands of dollars of furniture that they needed and wanted. Six months later one of Joe's customers come into buy the discontinued set. They never received a phone call from Joe. What do you think they thought of Joe in that moment? The words unprofessional and apathetic come to my mind. I could write an entire book just on this but we must move on.

# 28. Your Library

The list of marketing, sales and copywriting geniuses I am about to share with you is by no means a comprehensive list. Instead it's my personal list of people who have impacted me through their writings and books. Some are old and some are new but all are talented with a great message that you can benefit from. You cannot go wrong reading and studying them.

- John F. Lawhon
- Dale Carnegie
- Gerry Morris
- David Ogilvy
- Nido Qubein
- W. Clement Stone
- Zig Zigler
- Dale Carnegie
- Napoleon Hill
- Brian Tracy
- Seth Godin
- Dan Kennedy
- Gary Vaynerchuk
- Michael Gerber
- Robert Ringer
- David Sandler
- J. Douglas Edwards
- Paul Castain
- Simon Aronowitz

- Claude Hopkins
- Amy Porterfield
- Eben Pagan
- Sean Malarkey
- Gary Halbert
- Al Ries
- Jeff Johnson
- Joe Sugarman
- James Wedmore
- Victor Schwab
- Eugene Schwartz
- Jeffrey Gitomer
- Jack Trout
- Elmer Wheeler
- Mark Victor Hansen
- Dan Cricks
- Ron Sheetz
- Doug Stewart

"YES, THAT IS A GREAT IDEA!"

# 29. Idea of the Month

A good, effective marketer is never at rest. His marketing radar is always on. He is always looking at his numbers and making adjustments. He uses the right message, via the right media to the right person.

Another thing every smart marketer does is continually test new marketing ideas, promotions, messages and offers. Remember, what gets one person's attention, may not get another's.

I'm a fan of using a *"marketing calendar"* which allows me to schedule my marketing efforts in advance. By planning your marketing ahead of time, you can schedule in new campaigns and promotions. You might not know what they are in the scheduling phase, but the simple act of telling yourself you have an upcoming promotion scheduled, forces you to think. When I worked for Serta we had to submit a forecast for the next year which would eventually become a budget. There were categories for mattress stores, furniture stores, department stores, and other. When I first started, other was around 5% of my budget. When I left other was around 15% of my budget. We had to get creative and figure out what other would be. This was in the early 90s right before we started selling Sam's Club. I digress. Let's get back to marketing.

At a minimum, I would challenge you to develop a new marketing idea every month. That's only twelve a year and should be quite doable for everyone reading this book. Like the game of baseball, where even the best players have to be at bat a number of times before they get a hit, good marketing always requires you to be stepping up to the plate and taking swings.

# 30. Think Before You Act. Now Action!

All success-oriented business owners should be creative thinkers. This means they invest time and energy outside their work environment to dream up new product, service and marketing ideas. During this creative thinking process, employee/customer/electronic interruptions should be non-existent.

Do what you must to create a creative thinking environment to allow your analytical and creative brain *"to open up and breathe."* If that means coming into your store very early in the morning then do it. Some people need to change the scenery to get the creative juices going. I love lakes. My best thinking is always done next to water. I know some marketers who lock themselves in a hotel room and leave their phone in the car until their creative work is done.

While thinking and creative thinking about your business is very important, it's worthless without the second and critical part of the equation – **ACTION**!

The number of world-changing ideas that never happened, because the person who dreamt it up did not follow through, is countless. And I am guilty of this too so don't beat yourself up. Just commit to yourself that you are changing it right now. From this moment on take action and get'r done!

You've heard clichés like *"paralysis by analysis"* and even Helen Keller said *"Ideas without actions are worthless."*

The bottom line is thinking and subsequent action are forever linked together for the store owner on the road to success. Take time on a regular basis to think. When your thoughts are crystal clear write all out the steps and then take ACTION!

# 31. Not You!

This chapter, at first glance, may seem like the biggest contradiction in this book. I mean we're talking about marketing, so why wouldn't everybody potentially be our customer?

Simply because it's not possible and more importantly many people are not meant to be your customer. Unless you have unlimited resources and products that are universally accepted by every consumer as desirable. And those two conditions do not exist. Remember the previous chapter where I discussed your ideal target market?

That's the person who you want to invest your marketing budget in trying to attract, while at the same time repelling people who you're not able to help. Read that again. Did I say repel? Yes I did.

This efficiency allows you to do everything you can to help the people you can best help with your products and services, while not wasting efforts and resources on those your products and services cannot help. The more attention and money you can focus on the people your business is designed to do business with, the more successful you will be. Get it? Got it? Good!

I understand this may feel a bit uncomfortable at first, but it's fair to everyone involved when you're crystal-clear on who you can and cannot help. This will change over time but you need to start somewhere. Always measure and evaluate your customer's buying habits and what they are responding to. When possible find out why as well. It will help you to evolve with your customer instead of evolving away from your customer.

# 32. Five Marketing Laws

The following may sound a bit harsh, but they are fundamental human (and marketing) laws.

**Law #1**: People are not interested in you, or your product, or your service. They're only interested in what you, your product, or your service can do for them. All they really care about is what you can do to make their lives easier, better, or more enjoyable.

**Law #2**: People don't buy what they need. They buy what they want. People don't want you to sell them a product. They want you to solve their problem.

**Law #3**: It's up to you, the marketer of your business, to align the emotional *"reasons why"* your product or service can solve the pains (or fulfill the desires) of your ideal target customer and get that message in front of them in the most effective way possible.

**Law #4:** Marketing is a process, not an event. It never stops and only evolves and changes as dictated by the market.

**Law #5**: Good, effective marketing starts with you!

# 33. Your #1 Product Is You!

Successful store owners understand and embrace the fact that their #1 product is their own self, therefore they invest the time and money in making "*this product*" the best it can be.

In today's business world, there's no room for weak, personality-less, timid marketers and you must understand only the strong survive. Success starts with you, what you focus on, how you think and what you do on a repeated and consistent basis.

The good news is there are plenty of excellent books, courses and people to help you develop and maximize your personal skills and my goal with this chapter is to simply remind you of the critical importance on focusing on self-development. I am filty four years old right now. By the time I get this book finished and published I will be fifty five years old. I listen to most of my books in my van while I drive twenty to thirty hours a week. I have turned my van into a learning institution. I suggest that you find time and make time to further your sales, business, and marketing education.

When you accept the fact that like product research and development, personal research and development is equally important, you're on your way to bigger and better things. Here are a few simple ways to do this:

- Read, study and implement!
- If you drive a lot, it is listen and implement!
- Have an inner circle of trusted friends
- Attend events with excellent speakers
- Promise yourself you will always be a student
- Always be learning
- Celebrate and enjoy success, but be careful of complacency

# 34. Business Card Tips: Powerful Pocket Marketing

It's tough to imagine a marketing tool that's more versatile, portable, affordable, and readily accepted than a business card. The ubiquitous 3.5 inch by 2 inch piece of paper is used throughout the world.

When you can get 2,000 premium cards for well under $100, the "*bang for the buck*" is considerable and add that low cost to the personal nature of the medium, and you have a VERY attractive marketing tool every business owner should be using.

However, most people give little thought how to maximize their effectiveness and how to use them, in specific ways, to generate business. If you're still using a traditional, one-sided, paper business card that simply contains your contact information, you're missing out.

Because business card use is so common, the next three chapters are dedicated to specific business card marketing strategies, which are super easy to implement.

# 35. Business Card Tips: Don't Use Free Cards

I know, the offer is tempting and *"it's only a business card,"* right?

Wrong!

Free business cards, which typically have some sort of marketing promotion from the printer on the back (hence the reason they're free), like such as, *"Business cards are free at..."* are not acceptable for use in your business. It's your business not the company who gave the free business card's business.

What's your first impression when somebody hands you one of these numbingly boring, plain-vanilla cards? I doubt it's something positive and worth remembering.

When I've received similar cards, it doesn't exactly give me a vote of confidence in their business or how well they're doing.

First impressions are indeed important and the last thing you want to do is undermine a potential relationship because of your business card. In the end, free business cards will end up costing you money. Don't use them!

# 36. Business Card Tips: Create Specific Cards

Quality business cards are inexpensive to print and you can get them made in a matter of a few days. Given these two facts, a key strategy is to create specific business cards for specific reasons. *Attending an industry event?* Why not print specific cards just for that event? Here's a powerful idea. On the second side of the card, put the name of the event, and then print a message like *"Here's what we discussed..."* and leave the rest of the back side blank. That way the person receiving it can write in a short note to jog their memory after the event.

Maybe you print up cards for a specific promotion or sale. The possibilities are endless. Ask yourself this important question: *"When I hand somebody a card – what is the one single action I want them to take?"* When this book is complete, it will be on the back of my business card until my next book is published. If I owned a furniture store I would have the URL with an image of a short book on how to shop for furniture or better yet, "The 9 Biggest Mistakes Furniture Shoppers Make & How To Avoid Them". Get creative and have fun with it. Remember your marketing over time changes and gets better as you analyze your results and tweak your offers and marketing messages to better serve your customers, and most importantly yield a higher return on your investment. Consider creating business cards where you:

- Make a special offer
- Offer a free report, CD or gift
- Create an invitation for joint-venture partners
- Ask for referrals

# 37. Business Card Tips: Double the Power

This last idea can make your simple little business card into a powerful marketing weapon (and one I've already alluded to in the previous chapter).

I highly recommend every business card you print be a double-sided business card (with printing on both sides). By doing this, you've immediately doubled the amount of space to have a clear, relevant marketing message AND because most people don't do this, your card will stand out!

Believe it or not, I've seen business owners take this notion of a multi-sided business card to an extreme by creating business cards with four and even eight panels, in essence creating a *"mini brochure"* the size of the typical business card.

You can include things like a special offer, free gift or a discount to get somebody to follow-up with you after they have received your card. Making it some sort of *"call to action"* is very smart. Just about any business card printer can print a double-sided card for you and the additional cost is minimal.

# 38. Capture & Use Emails

You may already be building a mailing list, either in-house or through direct mail, events, and other promotions, but are you using that opportunity to collect email addresses? If you aren't, adding one simple line to your response form will increase the value of your database. In fact, some people are more likely to join a list if they can provide an e-mail address rather than a home address, so you have the opportunity to build an even larger list.

Collecting and then using emails on an on-going basis (at least weekly emails) is an important *"stay in touch"* strategy. Sprinkle in news, helpful tips, customer success stories and promotions in your emails to engage readers. Here are smart strategies for collecting email addresses:

- Ask for permission to send e-mails
- Let customers know to expect, frequency, etc.
- State your privacy policy
- Let customers know they can unsubscribe from your list at any time
- Send confirmation email when they join your list
- Send on-going communications to keep your business top-of-mind
- Send a monthly e-zine to foster a sense of community

# 39. Celebrate!

One of the smartest things you can always be doing with your marketing is to showcase and celebrate your customer success stories using your products and services. You can do this by writing about it and showing pictures in your customer newsletter, emails, video marketing, books, brochures, etc.

Recognition is one of the most powerful motivational forces, possibly second only to fear. If you sell furniture, it's about making a house a home. If you sell mattresses, it's about helping your customers waking up happy and pain free.

It's important to remember that the majority of your customers do NOT get outstanding results - mostly because they don't do anything, or don't follow your instructions. If you permit them to judge you and the value of what you offer based on their own experience, you'll lose them as fast as you get them.

Instead, you must show people who are succeeding, so that they judge based on those other peoples' successes and realize success with your products/services is possible and they can do the same. You should overwhelm them with success stories and positive testimonials.

# 40. Celebrate Your Business Anniversary and Other Special Events

Throughout the year, you'll want to personalize your business and allow prospects and customers a *"peek behind the curtain"* by celebrating anniversaries, birthdays and milestones unique to your business. While these special events don't have anything specific to do with your prospects and customers, they do give you a good (and fun) reason to run a beneficial marketing promotion. Remember that bit about segmenting your list?

What if you segmented your list by salesperson? What if you sent an email to all of Sally's customers a day or two before her birthday? Do you think the customers would have fun with that? What would your customers think about you as a store owner who values their salespeople. What would Sally the salesperson think? Good questions, huh? What if customers came into the store with a birthday card or wish for Sally? Could one of Sally's teammates take a picture and post it on your store's Facebook page? Maybe print that with a pic in your monthly newsletter? Would that create customer engagement? Yes, it would!

The point is to humanize and personalize your business so that it stands out from your competition and makes you unique and valuable to your customers. It also allows you to have a bit of fun with your marketing and there's definitely nothing wrong with having fun and putting a smile on someone's face. Here are a few promotional ideas to consider:

- Your business start anniversary
- Years in business promotion
- Team member birthday promotions
- X number of sales/customers promotion

- *"My son/daughter graduated"* promotion
- Special business or industry milestones
- Favorite Charity Promotion
- Do you have cute young children?
- They should be in your marketing
- Do you have pets?
- They should also be in your marketing

# 41. You Want Me To What?

Having marketing that works and creating a flood of new prospects in your business is worth nothing if you cannot convert them into sales. If you rely on any type of face-to-face interaction and you have others working for you in this capacity, it is imperative that you choreograph your sales process.

Everything from the greeting someone receives when they enter your place of business, to answering questions, to taking the order and to delivering the product or service should be scripted out and specific language should be used to help the customer in the best way.

This does not have to be overly complex or "*salesy*", but as the store owner, it is your responsibility to make sure your prospects and customers are getting the best you can deliver. Simply leaving it up to your employees to say the right thing is not the way successful stores are built. Let your salespeople participate in the scripting. Let them have ownership in this process. Your script should evolve over time. Weekly sales meetings where success stories are shared should guide this process.

Spend some time looking at your processes and write down how and what should be said at various points. Create an employee manual or sales guide and make sure everyone who comes into contact with a prospect or customer knows what their responsibilities are. Quarterly meetings with your sales team should provide an opportunity to modify the script in a structured way. The $64,000 question should be asked, "Is there a better way to ask this or do this that will get a better result?" Sales scripts that salespeople have ownership in can produce outstanding results.

"I THINK THE GUY FROM THE
FURNITURE STORE IS LOOKING
FOR YOU HON."

# 42. Create Bounce-Back Offers

Amongst veteran marketers, it's known as "*bounce-back marketing.*" A bounce-back is a follow-up offer that's sent to a customer along with a product that has already been ordered. You've seen these before when a product you ordered is delivered with an insert, coupon or catalog. It's an easy-to-implement strategy and the goal is to have the customer "*bounce back*" and order additional products and become a more valuable (and consistent) customer. It's a smart strategy because the cost is minimal to present the new offer(s) and the offer is being made to a qualified, current customer. That second point should not be quickly dismissed, since the best customer to sell something new to is an existing happy customer.

It doesn't have to stop with a physical product... recently I was eating with my family at a restaurant and during our meal the manager came over, asked us how our meal was and then offered us a substantial, "*limited time*" coupon to return to the restaurant in the future. Smart! Customers who bought a bedroom set could be offered a special offer on a nightstand. If a customer bought a sofa set by itself, an offer could be sent for tables and lamps. If a customer bought a mattress set by itself an offer could be sent about frames, protectors, pillows, and/or sheet sets. The list is endless - just use your imagination. To make this simple create offer delivery methods to coincide with processes you already have in place, like:

- Including the offer with delivery of their product
- Including the offer along with an invoice
- Including the offer as a newsletter insert
- Hand out the offer during a face-to-face sale

"THIS IS SPARKY, OUR
CUSTOMER LOYALTY MANAGER."

# 43. Paying For Loyalty!

Rewarding loyal customers is a smart strategy many different types of business owners can leverage with a simply loyalty program. While there are many loyalty-program service providers available to you, you can create your own simple one to encourage repeat business by creating a simple *"punch-out card"* that gets punched out every time they purchase.

You've seen this many times and it doesn't have to be fancy. One key strategy is to give a bonus credit on the first purchase as a reward for signing up. Keep in mind that most consumers have many of these types of cards and forgetting about them is quite common. Make sure you ask all customers, at the time of purchase, if they are a loyalty club member and get them to enroll if they aren't. Everyone else does it. Why not furniture & mattress stores?

You can also create an email rewards program, where you capture their email and/or cell phone information and send them frequent incentives to return to your business.

A combination of both a loyalty card and an email program will yield the greatest results. In any case, you want to get the customer's explicit permission to sign them up for your loyalty club.

"I USUALLY KNOW, SOMETIMES, EVERY NOW AND THEN, WHERE THE LATEST MARKETING PROMO IS, I THINK."

# 44. Create Systems

This is one of those strategies entire books have been written about. While I don't have that kind of space, if I can simply get you thinking differently, I've accomplished my goal. According to the dictionary a system is *"any formulated, regular or special method of procedure."*

In your business and specifically in your marketing, you need to create systems ways of doing things in your business that happen over and over again, with or without you, 24 hours a day, 7 days a week, rain or shine. When this happens, you have a system that is working for you all the time.

You need to have a lead generation system that captures qualified prospects information and follows up with them with specific marketing sequences.

You need to have a new customer system.

You need to have a *"lost customer"* system.

These are just a few of the marketing systems you need in your business, which are typically built with software systems (like a CRM) and traditional face-to-face interactions. Look at your business and determine what you can systematize and automate and then do it!

# 45. Do Direct Mail

Direct mail is one of the most effective ways to get your marketing message delivered, seen and read. In today's hyper-technology world, direct mail may seem outdated, but smart marketers know differently. Every business owner should be using direct mail in various ways and successful marketers know the best way to use direct mail is with multi-step campaigns (meaning multiple pieces get mailed over a short period of time). Do you know who one of the largest users of direct mail is? Google. That's right, Google. If you are not using direct mail you are missing a golden opportunity.

One important way is to use direct mail for finding new customers via a lead-generation campaign. This is where you purchase a "*cold list*" of leads from a company like InfoUSA, or use something like Every Door Direct Mail from the U.S. Postal Service, and send a multi-step direct mail campaign to the list, offering them some type of irresistible offer to respond. The keys to success with this type of campaign are:

- Knowing "*who*" you want to respond and what you want them to do

- Buying or renting a quality list that has a high chance of having many of these "who's" on it

- Creating eye-catching, benefits-laden pieces

- Sending out a sequence over a short period of time

- Tracking and adjusting as necessary

- Generally speaking unless you are extremely promotional you are looking for homeowners

# 46. More Direct Mail

Lead generation is not the only type of direct mail you should be doing on a regular basis. You should also be using direct mail to stay in touch with prospects and customers. One smart way to accomplish this effectively, as I discuss in another chapter, is the use of a customer-oriented print newsletter.

Remember this important truth. *It's not your customer's or prospect's job to look for reasons to stay in contact with you. It's your job to stay in contact with them.*

So many business owners forget this and leave way too much money on the table, simply because they're not staying in touch with their prospects and customers and letting them know about special promotions and other reasons why they should buy/stop back in/get a gift, etc.

Every month, you should be sending at least one if not two or three, direct mail pieces out. One should be your newsletter. The others could be simple postcards with a strong call-to-action, sales letter or even a greeting card if around a holiday.

Keep your direct mail focused on your prospects and customers wants and needs, suggest how you can help them and give them a clear, simple way to get the help. It's literally that simple to do good direct mail.

# 47. Do Off-Beat Promotions

*"Life's too short to be boring."*

I'm not sure who first said that, but I doubt it was a business owner, given the huge amount of boring and plain-vanilla marketing that is around all of us. For the smart marketer, this is a huge opportunity to have some fun, get attention and make more money by doing *"off-beat"* promotions that stand out and get noticed. This may feel uncomfortable and unnecessary, but I would challenge you to challenge yourself to go outside your comfort zone and doing something different that reflects your store's personality. Yes stores have a personality whether you want to believe that or not. Remember the worst sin in marketing is to be boring.

If you're stumped on what type of offbeat promotions to come up with, there are several books and web sites out there that can help you. One book you should read is *"Outrageous Advertising That's Outrageously Successful"* by Bill Glazer. Consider these *"outrageous"* ideas to get you started:

- Create marketing promotions around lesser known holidays. There are literally hundreds of "recognized" holidays throughout the year. One of my dealer's most successful campaigns was built around National Jelly Bean Day!

- Create fun and attention-grabbing videos and post on YouTube, your website and social media channels.

- Hire *"picketers"* to picket your low prices/great service etc. outside your location.

# 48. Create a Contest!

Contests have been around for decades because they work. You have to look no further than the lottery to understand the psychology why contests are so effective for getting people to engage and respond. Creating a good contest can build your prospect list, drive people to visit your store, buy your products, refer your store and more.

Recently, online and Facebook™ contests have become popular and have the potential to go viral and rapidly spread. There are many resources to help you create contests quickly and inexpensively. Here's a quick list of ways you can use contests in your marketing efforts:

- Social media contest - to build your list
- In-store contests - to drive traffic
- Leave a comment on my blog contest - to drive SEO and social proof
- Buy a product contest – to increase sales
- Customer #x contest (e.g. the 1,000th customer) – to drive sales
- Referral contest – to drive referrals

Just make sure you keep things above-board and you're not violating any laws or regulations.

# 49. Leverage Social Media

How to profitably leverage social media is still a question mark for many store owners, yet it's social-proof power and reach cannot be denied. Therefore figuring out a social media strategy for your business is something you should do.

The best advice I can offer in this limited amount of space, if you're a not using social media today, is to go to Amazon.com and search for the latest books on the *"business use of social media."* Look for the books that have the best reviews and study those authors. My favorites are Sean Malarkey, James Wedmore, Paul Castain, Amy Porterfield, and Gary Vaynerchuk.

In the meantime, here are a few practical pointers for leveraging social media:

- Focus on creating relationships with people
- Offer valuable tips and advice and become a trusted resource
- Engage in conversations and articulate how you can help people improve their lives
- Focus 90% of your time on engagement
- Create a fun and informational Facebook Fan Page
- Use a lead-gen magnet to help you create a list
- Offer special promotions only available to your social media friends and never exceed doing this 10% of the time

We do the right thing all the time
even when it costs us money.

Everyone says it - We Live It!
Ask me how!

# 50. Make It Right

Mistakes happen. Blunders occur. Oversights crop up. Sooner later, something is going to happen that is going to disappoint a customer. Don't worry about it. Instead, focus on what happens next. I've discovered that if there's an issue with a customer - even if the issue wasn't our fault – You can never go wrong making it right. Taking responsibility and making the customer's comfort and satisfaction a priority, especially after something goes wrong, sends a message that they matter to you. It says that your business isn't just about selling a product or service; it's about solving their problem, making their life better and standing behind your business.

Empower your team members to make it right instantly. Let them know what they can and cannot do without checking with you first. Have this thought out and in place before something happens. As the owner, you should send a handwritten apology. It probably will be the first and only one that customer will ever get. Handle a blunder gracefully, because it's an opportunity to build some of the strongest customer loyalty you can earn! Remember this the faster you make it right the happier the customer will be. Train all your service people and that includes salespeople, that speed is king when working with a customer who needs our help.

The saying on the previous page is currently on top of my **"Do The Right Thing Bill of Rights"** and on top of my website. It is also on the back of my business cards. It is part of our corporate culture in our small sales company but it guides everything we do. I am a wholesale rep, so my business is different than your store's business. I am including this only to give you some inspiration for your store.

# 51. Free Publicity!

Local media, such as newspaper and magazine reporters and editors, radio and television producers and even local bloggers can help you spread the word about your business if you can give them something that's newsworthy and beneficial to their readers, listeners and viewers.

The key is to be able to help them provide newsworthy, useful and beneficial information to <u>their customers</u> and not blatantly advertise your business.

Spend some time putting together a list of possible local media contacts. You can easily do this research on the web or you can contact a local publicity firm to do it for you.

I've seen many local business owners get unbelievable local exposure, for free, by simply figuring out what is a newsworthy and helpful topic and sending to the right media contact. If this topic of getting free publicity is new to you, I would suggest getting a book or two on Amazon.com on the topic of "free publicity" and following the step-by-step process of tapping into this potentially huge opportunity.

# 52. Mail Handwritten Thank-You Notes

I want to share with you a business strategy that by itself, can have a dramatic and positive effect on your business. And get this, EVERYBODY reading this can immediately implement and use in their business... EVERY BODY!

It's the power of the simple, handwritten business thank you letter or card. I know business owners that use Thank You cards as a primary marketing strategy and their results are phenomenal! Think about it... who doesn't like to be appreciated and thought of? This is an extremely powerful emotion you should be tapping into regularly and to help you consider when to send thank you cards, here's a list of *"thank you opportunities."*

- When you get a new customer
- Upon delivery of your product or service
- When an existing customer makes a purchase
- When someone gives you a referral
- When a peer gives you helpful advice
- As a follow-up after a store visit or phone call

In John F. Lawhon's book, "Selling Retail" he described the difference between really good retail salespeople and the elite million dollar plus producers. The really good salespeople sent a Thank You to everyone who bought. The elite million dollar plus producer sent a Thank You to everyone they worked with whether they bought or not. As a retail salesperson working for someone else I wrote Thank You notes on my own stationery with my own envelopes. It made a huge difference in my business. Four years after I left my last retail job customers were still asking for me according to my friends who still worked there.

# 53. Max Each Sale

Offering quality upsells is a fast and simple way to increase your revenues and profits, yet many business owners miss this opportunity to increase the value for the customer while increasing the overall purchase amount. An upsell is nothing more than having a variety of different options and/or quality levels that go along with the initial product purchase. You see it every time you set into a fast-food restaurant when they offer you the option to *"super-size"* your order.

Often business owners think you need a complex strategy for increasing your average dollar sale with new marketing efforts and lots of process re-engineering. In reality you can make up selling part of your sales process as easily as they do it in the fast food industry, just get your salespeople to ask if your customers want that extra something that makes their life easier or more enjoyable.

Making sure your salespeople are offering tables and lamps with their sofas and sectionals are obvious upsells that benefit both the consumer and the store. Salespeople should ask if the customer wants one nightstand or a matching pair?

When selling a mattress set there are numerous items that the consumer could benefit from. They are a new frame, new rails with ideal support, pillows and sheet sets. You are probably thinking I forgot about protectors and encasements. Did you think that? I didn't forget them. They are part of every mattress sale and therefore they are not an upsell. If a customer won't invest in a protector I simply would not sell them a mattress set. It's that important.

# 54. Profit with Packages

Packaging your products and services into bundles allows you to charge higher prices and creates the perception you're a premium store. It also provides a buying opportunity for the 5 – 20% of consumers who always purchase the highest priced option.

For example, let's say you own a furniture store. You can price a sofa or sectional at a higher than normal price but the customer can make it a complete room with tables and lamps at such a low price that they almost always purchase the bundle. This package would represent a substantial savings but it would also allow you to make more profit on every transaction. You're already in front of the customer for one service, so why not offer them a valuable package that would entice them to purchase more from you? This isn't new. Many great retailers have built entire businesses from this one strategy.

Even in the most competitive marketplaces you can package your products and services in a way that will allow you to charge a premium price. So, take the time today to sit down and come up with several different ways you can package your products and services to step your customers up into your higher product or service offerings. Use your imagination. Have fun with this!

# 55. Publish a Newsletter

The printed and mailed newsletter is, I believe, the most useful tool in maintaining relationships with customers and keeping them interested in you, your business, your products and services. Since "*publications*" get better readership than "*sales materials*" and "*articles*" get more readership than "*ads*," it makes profitable sense to put your messages into the format of a publication, like a customer newsletter and into the context of articles.

Sadly, many store owners are terribly lazy about this and never get their act together to put out a fun, quality and interesting newsletter every month. It's not hard and there are many books and resources to help you publish your own customer newsletter. Make sure your store's newsletter is fun. Do not commit the worst marketing sin of being boring. Make the newsletter about your customers 90% or more. Make the newsletter about your store less than 10%. Anything that is an upcoming community event should be featured. Remember the newsletter is a great tool to shape your customer's future behavior. So definitely thank customers publicly for behaviors that you want repeated. Those behaviors are testimonials, 5 star consumer site reviews, repeat business, and referrals. Have fun with your newsletter! Let your store's personality shine through. Here are a few content tips for your newsletter:

- Information/education directly linked to your products and services
- Photos of successful customers
- Customer recognition and appreciation
- Product and service promotions
- Recognize and stimulate referrals

- Any charity work your store is involved with
- Customer testimonials should always be modeled
- Quotes with pictures
- Recipes
- Contests
- Crossword Puzzles
- Cartoons
- Treating your employees well publicly

# 56. Oldies But Goodies!

I've seen a phenomena occur with many business owners over the years, where they STOP doing a marketing promotion that has worked for them in the past. I'm not sure if it's because they get bored with it or think they need to do something new.

Take some time and do an inventory of your past marketing promotions. Which ones have done exceptionally well? Which ones gave you the greatest return on investment?

Are you still using them? If so, great job!

If not, why not *"dust them off"* and start using them again?

Many times these old promotions simply need to be updated with the most recent language, pricing, benefits, etc. You've already done the hard work of creating it the first time, so do a quick update and send it out again!

If your business is multi-generational ask the older generations for ideas. They love sharing their knowledge but often won't unless asked. Ask them lots of questions in different ways so that you can mine some pure marketing gold.

The use of a marketing calendar to schedule promotions in advance helps track and remind you of all your marketing promotions available.

# 57. Sell Like Disney

If you've ever been to Disney World or Disneyland, you know just how masterful and intentional Disney is at selling and extracting as much money from guests as possible. Disney is bold and relentless when it comes to pricing and asking for the sale and therein lies the gold for business owners. Here are a few strategies I took away from my last visit to Disney World:

**Make it about the experience and not the price**. Does anybody do it better than Disney? Doubtful. Disney wraps everything they do with *"unique experience"* and it's a fundamental part of the Disney magic. It's how they charge almost $40.00 for a simple breakfast buffet that has random Disney character visits during your meal. By making it a memorable experience for the kids, the parents open up their wallets.

**Make it fun to do business with you**. Even the grumpiest tight-wad will manage a smile at Disney. A huge part of the Disney experience is about the fun memories they create for families and generation after generation of visitors attest it is indeed *"The Happiest Place on Earth."*

**Create a captive audience**. Disney has done a tremendous job at keeping guests in the Disney bubble during their entire visit. For example, we stayed at a Disney resort, took Disney buses and monorails, ate at Disney restaurants, shopped at Disney stores, etc. and during this time, we were exposed to many marketing messages and opportunities to buy. Can you do something similar in your business so when customers enter your world, you've captured their attention and focus? Membership sites and newsletters are simple ways to create a captive audience.

When you market with information and become the authority in furniture or mattresses, to your customers, you are putting them in your marketing bubble and eliminating competition.

**Offer many opportunities to spend money.** A Disney sales experience starts when you book your trip and does not end until you return home. In between you're presented with many different opportunities to spend money, Disney is not bashful when it comes to frequency and pricing. It's truly a spectacle to behold, but because they do such a great job at creating a special experience, nobody seems to notice. Next time you go to Disney just make peace with the fact that they are separating you from your money and look at it with new eyes. Want to make your money back tenfold? Look at Disney through the eyes of a marketer. Do not say, "But my business is different". Ask this question instead, "How can I adapt that idea to fit into my business?"

**Purchase in advance and save more**. Disney has studied human psychology and knows how to press the right buttons. One smart strategy is offering special savings on *"purchase in advance"* offers. For only a few hundred dollars more than what I spent on four, three-day passes, I could have received four annual passes that would allow unlimited visits to the Disney Parks for an entire year. Their slogan is *"The more you play, the less you pay per day!"*

So we are visiting Disneyland in two weeks and I can't wait to go! We as a family will make memories for a lifetime and that is the primary reason for going. I will drink up every second of that experience as I know at fifty four how precious life is. I have a confession to make. My inner marketer is going to have a field day! I will jot down at the end of every day all my marketing and business lessons that I learned at Disney so that I can pass them on to my dealers.

# 58. Sponsor an Annual Award in Your Community

Fostering good will in your local community is important for a local business for several reasons, the least of which is the publicity and marketing opportunities it can bring you. While you always want to have your marketing radar on, this is a time when you want to put your needs on the back burner and figure out ways to give back to your community. Make sure you are doing it for the right reasons. When you do, forces that you cannot imagine conspire to create a truly special event.

One strategy to accomplish this is to create and sponsor a special award (or awards) that recognize individuals, or companies or organizations for a specific reason (one that should be important to you). It's best if you can tie a personal story as to why this award exists and why it's important to you to create this recognition.

So, for example, if academics are important to you, you could sponsor an award for the high school student who showed the most improvement during the school year. Consider meaningful prizes that make sense and do the most good.

You can promote this award through the local media and get exposure for the award and your business.

# 59. Surprise & Delight Your Customers!

Any day, at any time, you have the power to surprise and delight a customer.

Remember to do it, and do it often. Get a reputation for giving something away—a product or a discount—when you don't have to. It's cheap marketing. Your customer will have his day pleasantly interrupted, he will tell a bunch of his friends, you will have increased your bond with him, and all of this will generate additional sales.

Your ability to do this is only limited by your imagination. For years I have taught and at times begged my retailers to call customers after their delivery to make sure they are happy with their purchase and the service they have received. A simple phone call goes a long way. Remember, it's all about making your customer feel appreciated and valued. Customers who feel appreciated buy again, give 5 star consumer site reviews, give testimonials, and gladly give referrals.

Please do not be limited by my simple example. Get creative and uncover more ways to surprise and delight your customers. Have fun with it!

# 60. Survey Your Customers

One of the most important things a business can do is to invest time to understand its customers. This can be accomplished in several ways, but by far the easiest and fastest way is to simply ask them. This simple, straightforward method can be done in a few different ways: by speaking to your customers one-on-one as they visit your store; by convening a small focus group of your customers; or by creating a survey and asking your customers to participate.

You can use a simple paper and ink survey or you can use a web survey system like SurveyMonkey.com. The purpose is to get important feedback on specific business questions. Here are a few survey tips:

- Define your goal

- Survey the right participants

- Reward their participation

- Craft strategic, easy-to-understand questions

- Thank them for participation

- Analyze and act on the results

- Communicate back to them the changes implemented.

- Thank them again.

Obviously this is just a quick look at survey strategies, but the important take-away is to periodically ask for specific feedback from customers (and prospects) for valuable business information. Customers who feel that they are part of your store's community will feel appreciated and become evangelists for your store.

# 61. Kodak Moments!

The use of photographs in marketing is typically under-utilized by store owners and it's a mistake. Photos are a great way to convey customer-success and they are an excellent way to engage people and help build community. You don't have to go to the expense of hiring a professional photographer to use photos in your business (however for certain types of photos that might be necessary) and often-times the more *"down and dirty"* approach of a simple cellphone photo is more effective and realistic. Here are several different types of photos you can use in your marketing efforts:

- Pictures of happy customers

- Pictures showing the reward of using your stuff

- Pictures showing the effect of <u>NOT using</u> your stuff

- Before and after photos

- Enlarged photos detailing your product

- Pictures of you with happy customers

- Pictures of employees with happy customers

- Historical or legacy photos

- Happy customers getting their delivery

- Customers flashing the thumbs up

- Action pictures of you and your staff with your happy customers

- Happy customers holding an I Heart Symbol Your Store's Name Sign

- Happy employees with happy customers

# 62. Promote Your Store

Everybody is familiar with promotional items, like the ubiquitous custom-imprinted pens and many reading this might dismiss the power of promotional items, which would be a mistake. Done right, using promo items in your marketing can increase your business and brand awareness, visibility and create a *"sticky factor"* that reminds people of your business. Unfortunately most business owners use promotional items in a haphazard way and don't get the full benefit they offer. Remember promotional items can sell twenty four hours a day seven days a week. Here are a few ideas to consider when using promotional marketing items.

- Find products that are useful. Every time they use it, they remember you. The one item my dealers love the most are small pads of paper that fit in a retail salesperson's pocket. My contact information is listed. It is the single most requested item that I have ever giving away.

- Include your name (personal, company, product, etc.) and phone number and/or web address on the imprint

- Consider including a call-to-action on the imprint

- Shop around – the promotional items business is a competitive one and shopping could save you money

- The stylus pens are popular right now (Sept. 2015)

- My pens have only my name, website, and phone #

- Magnets that are decent quality have great staying power on your customer's refrigerator. Don't make it a business card. Follow the advice on yellow pages. Start with a question.

# 63. Tell A Story

Storytelling is one of the oldest human rituals and is a strategy important to your marketing efforts. Few business owners understand this and those that do and use stories in their marketing will reap amazing results. Stories are an important element in connecting your message with your audience and getting them remembered. We humans process information much more efficiently when it's in the form of a story and we're therefore much more likely to remember it.

We quickly forget a dry recitation of the facts. Yet, most marketing is just that: fact after fact after fact ... *"buy this widget from us, and it'll do this, this and this"*

That doesn't stick.

If you want your marketing to connect at an emotional level, if you want people to remember it, you need to turn your marketing messages into stories. Here are a few story-starter ideas you can use to connect with people:

- Stories about your life and why you started your business

- Stories about your struggles and accomplishments

- Customer success stories

- *"Teachable moment"* stories

Remember your goal is to connect and convey a message in a friendly and engaging way that will stick with the customer.

"HAVE YOU EVER HEARD OF
COPYDOODLES?"

# 64. Handwriting Magic!

Getting attention in your marketing is important and an effective way to do this is with the use of simulated handwriting on your print and web marketing. In this day and age of computer-generated everything, the power of handwriting stands out and gets noticed. You cannot help but see this technique used more and more. It's in the advertisements in your weekend paper; it's on television commercials, in magazine ads and on web sites.

So why is simulated handwriting so effective? Quite simply, the widespread use of computers, word processing and laser printers has created *"homogenized marketing."* Meaning 95% of everything looks the same. When you introduce a handwritten or hand-drawn element to the mix, it becomes very different in a simple, human-personality kind of way.

The effectiveness of a simple red handwritten note that says something like *Special Sale Price"* cannot be beat. Same with the use of hand-drawn shapes and doodles. They stick out, get noticed and get read. All critical for eventually making the sale.

The easiest way to add handwriting and hand-drawn doodles is with a product I highly recommend called CopyDoodles®. Any business owner can easily use CopyDoodles and you can learn more at http://www.CopyDoodles.com. Remember the greatest marketing sin is being boring. Nothing beats CopyDoodles to engage your customers and draw them into your compelling story/message. Pardon the pun.

# 65. Instant Recognition

The World Wide Web, as we know it, has been around for almost two decades and it's not going away anytime soon. Yet with almost 20 years of opportunity, I'm still amazed at how many business owners I see using generic or boring URLs in their business. You can register a domain for less than $1.00 for an entire year, so why wouldn't you tap into the unique attention-grabbing power of a benefit-driven domain?

What's a benefit-driven domain you might ask?

It's a memorable URL who's only job is to get people to notice and visit the site because it appeals to and intrigues them. It articulates a clear benefit or message and is uniquely different that a domain that is simply a company or product name. When a person visits the URL, it takes them to a focused web page. Here are a few benefit-driven domain examples to illustrate this concept:

www.GetYourFreeBook.com

www.SaveOnTaxes.com

www.GetACleanHouseTomorrow.com

See the difference? Each of these articulates a benefit that appeals to the target recipient and to maximize effectiveness, each should drive people to a very specific, benefits-oriented web page offer.

# 66. Write Blog Posts For SEO

I can make a very strong case why every business web site should have a blog component to it and the three main ones are:

- To write informative articles for your target market.
- To create search engine optimization (SEO) *"juice."*
- To engage your customer and position yourself as the authority

Each of these requires a much deeper study than what I can do here, but know if you don't have a blog where you can write frequent, timely and benefit-oriented articles targeting specific *"keywords"* around your business, industry and customers wants, you're missing out on an important connection strategy and way to get free search engine rankings on sites like Google and Yahoo.

I can write a blog post on a specific topic I know my readers are searching for, post it and within a few hours get a high ranking on Google (as in page 1 or page 2 depending on the keywords I was targeting). If you already have a blog, you need to start writing blog posts (a.k.a. articles) that are written around a very specific keyword or keywords you know people are looking for. If you own a local business, you would also want to include your town or location. For example, a restaurant owner could write an article on his homemade pasta recipe around the keywords *"best pasta in New York"* and when people search for pasta in New York, her article could be one of the top pages ranked in the search engine. There are plugins that will help you with your SEO. Just Google top SEO plugins and spend a few minutes researching them. This will help you save time which is something that is near and dear to every store owner's heart.

# 67. Become a Trusted Authority

Nothing beats being a published author to create an unmatched level of influence, credibility and expertise proof. Whether it's a printed book, digital book or special report by becoming an author, you instantly rise above the 95% of business owners who are not authors, which gives you distinct advantage. You can get free publicity by promoting your book to the local news media, promote local *"evening with the author"* events and much more when you've become an author.

Hate to write? You can speak your book into existence and then have it transcribed. You will need to have someone polish it for you. Spend lots of time thinking about the questions you need to be asked. There is a book in everyone. Share your knowledge with the world. Just do it!

# 68. Your Customer Is A V.I.P.!

While it goes way beyond the boundaries of this book, if I can give you a spark to think this through a bit more, it could be a huge game-changer for you.

Wrapping your products or services into a paid membership program can generate monthly or annual continuity income. So instead of simply making a one-time sale, your first sale leads to a stream of monthly or annual sales (depending on your membership model).

I've given this idea to many business owners who have a business that could be expanded with the implementation of a paid membership program and 95% of the time, they nod their heads and forget about it as soon as we're done talking. BIG MISTAKE!

A membership program targeted to your best customers will keep them connected to you and coming back (or using what you sell) over and over again. In its most simple form, a membership program is a bundle of products or services that when totaled are worth far more than the monthly or annual membership fee.

I've seen V.I.P. membership programs work in restaurants, salons, auto-repair shops and in a variety of retail businesses. I've even seen a plastic surgeon create a V.I.P. membership program. Spend some time thinking about what you can wrap into a membership program. Yes furniture and mattress stores can do this. Just start to think about it and someday the light bulb will go off. This one suggestion can pay incredibly huge dividends.

"WOW, YOU'RE GOOD!"

# 69. Hire a Mystery Shopper

*"Inspect What You Expect."*

Employees and team members are inherently critical for many businesses. If you have them, you know the health and profitability of your business is directly related to how employees and team members are interacting with each other, your customers and vendors. Therefore it's critical you have a system in place to inspect what is going on in your business when you're not explicitly watching.

One way to accomplish this is to hire *"mystery shoppers."* Hired as independent contractors, mystery shoppers are *"posers"* operating in stealth-like fashion to assess your business operations. They are charged with specific tasks such as taking photographs, purchasing a product or service, returning a product, registering complaints, asking questions of salespeople and behaving in other ways similar to how a real customer would act.

The whole point is to inspect how your employees and team members are interacting with your customers. Are they doing the right things? Are they saying the right things? The mystery shoppers will then report back to the business owner with details about their experiences. Many times, the results are scary. Be prepared to be shocked at what you discover.

Do a web search on *"mystery shoppers"* to learn more about creating your own system or hiring a professional firm to do it for you. Read "No B.S. Ruthless Management of People and Profits: No Holds Barred, Kick Butt, Take-No-Prisoners Guide to Really Getting Rich" by Dan Kennedy for more ideas on inspecting what you expect.

# 70. Create Your Own Holiday

Everybody loves celebrating holidays and it should come as no surprise to the reader that marketers around the world have figured out ways to drive business and increase sales with holiday marketing.

While the classic holidays celebrated in various cultures typically honor a momentous event or person, there's no reason you cannot tap into the marketing power of holidays by creating your own holiday to celebrate a single day or even a month. One related to your business, products, services, industry, etc.

A quick web search for *"fun holidays"* or *"unique holidays*

A dentist could create *Sparkling Teeth Day.*

Are you celebrating May is Better Sleep month? If not, wake up. A mattress store could create *Pain Free Sleeping Month.* A furniture store could create "Recliner Month" or "Put Your Feet Up Month" to include all reclining furniture.

You get the idea. The only thing you need to create your own holiday is a bit of creativity and the follow-through to just do it. I know I keep saying but please have fun with this! Life is way too short not to find joy in your work.

# 71. Create Raving Fans With Delivery!

Is your delivery of your store's products an exceptional and memorable experience? If not make it one. I once worked for a mattress company that allowed their delivery people to wear tank tops in the summer. So everything was professional about the experience till the end. In my humble opinion we failed our dealers by not having a professionally dressed delivery person make the delivery.

Remember, success in business in the 21st century is very much about being personalized, exceptional and doing the things 95% of your competitors aren't doing. So if everybody in your industry delivers the final product one way, you do it a different and better way. One that stands out and gets noticed.

This doesn't have to be expensive and difficult to do. I know of one mattress store retailer who leaves a fun and unique gift bag on top of every new mattress they deliver. It contains homemade treats, a survey card, a few referral card and a few other fun things. Do you think this reaffirms the new mattress owner made the right buying decision? Absolutely! How about rolling out a red carpet for delivery? They do that too!

If you do in-house delivery, make sure your delivery team is well-dressed, clean, professional and on-time. Consider leaving a nice gift behind. If you ship your product, include some unexpected gifts in the package that makes your customer smile.

# COMPLAINTS

"YES, I HAVE A PROBLEM!
YOU PEOPLE REMEMBER MY
WIFE'S BIRTHDAY BETTER THAN ME!"

# 72. Send Birthday Cards

Did you know there's one *"holiday"* that's most celebrated around the world and one we can all use in our marketing... THE BIRTHDAY! Think about it... every one of your customers, clients, patients or prospects has a birthday, which gives you a reason why to not only contact them, but to offer them something special for their special day.

Furniture and mattress stores can benefit from a birthday marketing program. What does matter is that you see the value and applicability to creating a birthday marketing program. A customer relationship management system will enable you to send out birthday cards. Here are a few tips to get started.

Tip #1: Collect birthday information. No need to get too personal here, simply ask for their birth-month and birth-day during the sales process. You can use a software system to remind you when to send out an email or card in the mail.

Tip #2: Send out a personalized birthday email on their birthday. Wish them well. Use a fun, quirky picture. Add a special birthday offer to have them come back into your business.

Tip #3: Make your own birthday card and mail it. You can come up with a fun, uniquely different birthday card you mail to your customers on their special day. While it's not absolutely necessary, I would highly recommend you give them a special birthday gift to get them to do more business with you.

So an on-going birthday card campaign is not a difficult or expensive effort. People will appreciate it and it will definitely set your business apart from the competition.

# 73. Offer Free Educational Seminars

You've heard it before... *"an educated customer is the best customer."* In this day and age of countless choices, options and competitors, a smart way to distinguish your business is by helping your customers become better educated about what it is you offer.

One unique way to accomplish this is by holding free seminars, classes and educational events built around your products and services. You can hold these during the day or evening, either at your store or a local hotel or community hall.

The idea behind these educational events is to create and enhance the relationship and to put yourself and your business in a category of one. Nothing can improve the customer relationship like the ability to connect with them in a non-sales, benefits -driven, face-to-face experience. Few if any business owners get this, which is why I want you to do it.

No matter what it is you do, there is a 99% probability you can host a training/educational event to teach attendees the *"in's and out's"* of what it is you sell. You can educate them on what to look for and what to watch out for and though these are not *"selling events,"* your attendees should come to the logical decision your product or service is the right choice for them.

Please do not say, "But My Business Is Different" I can't do this because furniture and mattress stores don't do this. Go to Lancaster, PA and look for Gardner's Mattress & More. They do this and you can too!

# 74. Shop For Smart Marketing Tools and Resources

Success-oriented furniture and mattress store owners are marketers. They know the sustainability of their business is directly related to the quality and quantity of the marketing they do and the investments they make in various marketing tools and resources. The most successful business owners I know make a substantial and on-going investment in improving themselves, their marketing knowledge and their marketing arsenal. They are not afraid to spend money on tools and resources which will help them grow their business. <u>Nor should you</u>.

While there is a lot of junk out there, promoted and sold by charlatans, there are also a lot of things that can help you create better marketing, better systems and better results and you should be actively seeking them out.

- Subscribe to <u>quality</u> paid marketing newsletters

- Attend marketing seminars and workshops

- Read one or two marketing books a month

- Network with smart marketers

Don't have time to read? Listen to books, courses, and podcasts while you drive. Simply strive to be a *"lifelong student of marketing"* and you'll be amazed at the difference it will make in your business.

Earlier I talked about the power of masterminds. If you own a store you should belong to an industry mastermind and a marketing mastermind. Nothing could be more valuable than sharing ideas with smart capable people.

# 75. Turn Yourself into A Cartoon

*"Life's too short to be boring."*

If you're like me and don't yourself too seriously, this marketing tip is a real gem and one you can have a lot of fun with!

Turn yourself into a cartoon!

I don't have all the space needed to tell you why cartoons and comics are a smart marketing strategy, but just know they are powerful attention-grabbers and ways to engage people. I think every business owner should have his or her own cartoon. As soon as I finish this book I will take my own advice.

For little cost you can turn yourself into a cartoon character, a comic book hero or even an animated cartoon you can use on TV or in web videos. There's many different styles of cartoons, so do your research and see what you like best. You can hire a cartoon artist quite inexpensively on sites like www.guru.com and www.odesk.com. Or if you are cheap like me, you can use www.fiverr.com.

Another choice is to have your caricature drawn, which is a unique form of a cartoon designed to exaggerate your features. A smart strategy is to have your face and head drawn and then have the artist create various poses and holiday outfits and put your cartoon head on them for use throughout the year.

The bottom line is to have fun and connect in a fun and different way with your prospects and customers. People like to do business with people they know, like and trust and your own cartoon character can help accomplish this!

We do the right thing all the time
even when it costs us money.

Everyone says it - We Live It!
Ask me how!

# 76. Bill Of Rights

Simon Aronowitz helped me craft this for my dealers. I include it when I open a new dealer. I am the first rep in the furniture and mattress industry to do this. Would your customers benefit from their own Bill of Rights from your store? Here it is. I know you are sick of me saying this but have fun with this and let this serve as inspiration. your Bill of Rights will be much different than this one.

## Do The Right Thing Bill of Rights
### The New Bill of Rights For Dealers Who Demand More!

1. Right to Success. We are committed to helping you achieve it! You are never alone when you buy from Primeau Furniture Sales.

2. Right to Have Fun & Make Money!

3. Right to experienced and professional reps with retail sales experience who understand the furniture and mattress industry and who care about your business.

4. Right to the best selling and highest profit merchandise available in the marketplace, so you can close more sales and make more money!

5. Right to sell high quality products that your consumers will enjoy for years to come, quality products that will help you build loyal customers who continue to buy from you.

6. Right to speedy delivery of what you ordered.

7. Right to have your sales staff professionally trained to sell the products that you offer to your consumers.

8. Right to reps who can create ads and advertising campaigns for you including social media.

9. Right to be inspired by new and creative ideas and other dealers success stories that your reps bring to you on a regular basis.

10. Right to have product problems handled by a rep who cares in a prompt and professional manner.

11. Right to a rep who has your back.

12. Right to a rep who helps you to position your business as more than just a price and brand.

13. Right to be treated like a big dealer even when you are a little dealer.

14. Right to a rep who can help you create an enjoyable buying experience for your customers in your store.

15. Right to a mulligan when you need it. We have the clout with our vendors to color outside the lines every now and again to prevent you from losing money.

16. Right to dedicated office staff who are always working for you to ensure your complete satisfaction.

# 77. Start A Podcast

Start a podcast featuring answers to the most commonly asked questions that your customers ask you.. You can interview people or do a topic based podcast. Remember the worst sin in marketing? That's right, being boring. Podcasts allow the customers to hear your voice or even see you if it's a video podcast. How about a podcast with a local designer? Maybe a podcast with one of your sales reps with one of your higher volume lines?

Don't like your voice? Get over it! No one likes their own voice. There are famous broadcasters who hate their voice and despite that make millions of dollars with their voice.

I could write an entire book on podcasts but that is beyond the scope of this book. I can tell you one of the best things I have ever done in my business is starting my own podcast. Thank you to Paul Castain for pushing me and literally pushing me over the cliff when it came time to launch. You don't need a bunch of listeners. Just a few every month who become customers of your store.

There is lots of great free information out there. I started off with Pat Flynn's free information and ended up joining Podcaster's Paradise by John Lee Dumas. That was the single smartest thing that I could have ever done. So a big thank you to John Lee Dumas!

# 78. Your Traveling Billboard

Your truck is a traveling billboard. Are you marketing with it. Or is it plastered with your current vendor's logos? What happens when you change vendors? Do you repaint the truck or are you advertising for your competition?

Why not market your store? Maybe offer the customer multiple ways to get in touch with you? Maybe ask them a question that your customers ask themselves right before they become your customer?

The most valuable real estate on the truck is the back of the truck. Why? Because when you are at a stop light you will read the back of the truck. Put how to get your free report or book right on the back plus all the ways they can contact your store. It will pay huge dividends.

Look at this truck from my friends at Gardner's Mattress & More. Now that's a truck that sells!

# 79. Yellow Page Magic

Yellow pages are dead! You have either heard this or said this. It may or may not be true for your store. Before you run away from the yellow pages too quickly you need to ask yourself a question: Does my customer use the yellow pages?

If you sell goods and merchandise to the affluent you might want to be in the yellow pages. But not with a typical ad that looks like a business card. Your yellow page ad must have a compelling question which will serve a header. Boldly proclaim your store's USP. What makes you different must be featured so they cannot miss it!

Direct them to a download where they can get complete information about your store. At least more than can be fitted in a small yellow page ad. Use a special telephone number to the store that helps you track the ad's effectiveness.

Using a download to a free book can be very effective. Show up in unexpected places. Sure you can list your store under the furniture or mattress store headings. How about under sleep aids? My friends at Gardner's Mattress & More advertise under the Chiropractor heading. How about under "Beds" or "Adjustable Beds"?

# 80. Power In Motion

I am writing this on May 8, 2015. Right now there is a tidal wave in the mattress industry. It's called adjustable beds. Either you as a retailer will get with it or quite possibly be crushed by it. There is no reason not to get in the game that I can think of. Here is my seven step formula to winning with adjustable beds:

1. Merchandise a wide range of adjustable beds. If your mattress brand carries adjustable beds carry them.

2. Display adjustable beds under every mattress that you possibly can.

3. Market with information.

4. Advertise them consistently.

5. Train your salespeople every week if not every day on how to sell adjustable beds.

6. You must invest in trainers beyond what the manufactures provide. You need to pay a trainer that teaches your salespeople how to sell all your products not just some of them. Call me for a recommendation!

7. Train your service personnel, salespeople, and yes even the receptionist on the ins and outs of servicing adjustable beds. Train your receptionist to ask one question that eliminates most of your service complaints. This is worth the price of the book. Every trainer worth his or her salt will tell you that most of the complaints on adjustable beds will go away with one question. Here it is: "Is your bed plugged into the electrical outlet?"

# 81. Say No!

You must say no to the things that distract you away from your important work. You must say no to interruptions and infringements on your time.

You need to set boundaries for employees, vendors, media reps, and even charities. All of these groups are important to be sure. Tell your media reps and vendor reps that they must have appointments to see you from now on.

The days of them walking in on you are over. Be polite but firm. You will need to send a few out of your door because they forget your new policy. Be sure that you have spoken to them or emailed them about your new policy before you start enforcing it. You will only need to say no once and they will conform to your new policy as well. You are also doing them a favor by forcing them to be more organized.

# 82. Save The Parents!

Set up a play area for your customer's children. Your customers will absolutely love you for it. It doesn't need to be a large area loaded with a bunch of video games or expensive toys. This nothing new. My friend Nat Bernstein who just retired from Tempur-Sealy was in charge of playing with customer's children when he was eight years old at his Mother's furniture store!

It only needs to do a couple of things. One is keep the children occupied while their parents shop or often when Mom is shopping. The second is it needs to give Mom and/or Dad the peace of mind to focus on their new furniture or mattress. If you want visit the best play area that I have seen go to JV Schultz in Erie, PA! Tell John that I sent you.

It can be a small area. My dealers have created great play areas with old toys that their children no longer play with. I should have titled this chapter "Save Your Sale!" Why? Because distracted parents don't buy. If you are saying duh to me right now, I don't blame you. So allow me this one question. Do you have play area in your store?

# 83. Differentiate Or Die!

You as a retailer should not just blindly buy the same manufacturers as your competitors. There are some really great little known products that give your store great margins and your customers a great product.

Do your homework. Know all your competitors and the lines they carry. It's a lot of work. But it's work that must be done. Strive to have a store that looks different and feels different than your competitors. Most stores that you think are successful aren't. Go back and read that again. So don't copy them.

This entire book is about showing up differently than your competitors in your advertising, merchandising, display, sales training, and your service policy and procedures. Find a unmet need and fill that need for your customer.

When the Ellman family sold IBC years ago, they left a gaping hole in the industry that was never filled. Their customers called them imploring them to come back into the mattress industry. When their non-compete was up, the Ellman's in 2010 came back into the mattress industry. They more than filled the gap that no other company could fill and the result in less than five years is Sherwood Bedding, and they are tracking for well over $100 million in sales.

There is a gap in your marketplace. Find that gap and fill it better than any other store can.

"THE 'PUT ALL YOUR EGGS IN ONE BASKET STRATEGY' SEEMS TO WORK FOR HIM."

# 84. Too Many Eggs?

Do you have too many eggs in too few baskets? I am talking about vendors here. Have you ever experienced a vendor that turned cold? Ever had a vendor turn on you? It happens and when it does it can be disastrous for your business and your profits.

There is a fine line between carrying too many vendors and too few. Here are a few questions to ask yourself: Am I having trouble meeting the minimum shipping quantity on a regular basis? You might have too many vendors or the wrong vendor.

Does your vendor open new dealers in your marketing area with no regard for your business? If yes, that vendor probably needs to go. I qualify with this, are you giving your vendor a substantial amount of business? If yes you need to make sure the vendor is treating your business with the respect it deserves. Is your margin eroding with a vendor? This usually happens because of too much competition. I would voice my concerns to the vendor along with a timetable for correction. If uncorrected the vendor gets the boot.

# 85. The Secret To Eliminating Competition

The secret to eliminating your competition is to market to your customer with information instead of with price discounting. When you advertise with mass media do you know how many people are in the market at one time? It's between 1 to 5% for mattresses. If you market with an information offer you can start to capture your customer's attention before they are in the shopping stage. If your competitors only advertise to 1 to 5% of the market and you advertise to 100% everything else being equal who wins? That's right, you!

This allows you to shape the conversation and position your store as the authority and the expert. That's part of how you eliminate your competition. With your merchandising and display you can further differentiate your store from your competitors.

A customer focused sales process that is in sync with your advertising is the critical piece where many stores fall down. Your salespeople must know exactly what the customer has seen and heard from your advertising department so they can continue to deliver a consistent experience to the customer.

# 86. I Was Wrong!

I said around 2012 that the big long term finance offers were gone and they weren't coming back. Boy was I wrong! Not only are they back, they are bolder and longer than ever. Make sure that you have a few finance companies to offer different finance options to your customers. Every dealer who is serious about making money must become proficient in getting all their customers approved through one program or another.

You must have multiple finance companies that offer a range of products to your customers. You should have at least three. You must have a No Credit Check Company. You need a primary company that gives competitive rates to customers with good credit. You must have another company that will buy your primary company's turn-downs. If you are not using multiple finance companies you are cheating your store out of a lot of business and a lot of higher end more profitable business.

# 87. Alert...Alert...Alert

Google Alerts that is. How would like to have a team that worked for you around the clock? That delivered an intelligence report to your inbox? You can and it's free!

You can set up Google Alerts for you, your friends, your store, your competitors both retail and wholesale, your suppliers, and your industry. You can choose to have alerts emailed when they happen, daily, or weekly. I recommend daily. If you want to know right away, simply choose as it happens. If you don't want too many emails you may choose once a week.

Knowledge is power. The more you know about your competitors the better for you. It's important to know what is being said about you and your store. You need to see what is being said so you can be prepared. If you don't use Google Alerts you are cheating yourself. Set it up today!

# 88. Read Their Minds

I already talked about Google Alerts for specific information. Oftentimes as business owners we ask ourselves where is the market going? Where is it trending? Thanks to Google trends you can type in a keyword and see how it is trending for online searches.

Never forget the best consumer research is face to face when they are in your store I have repeated this often throughout this book on purpose. Ask customers all different questions. I will list a few here:

- How did you hear about us?

- Have any of your friends or family members bought here before?

- Thank you for your business! Why did you choose us?

- Was there one thing that you really liked about our store?

- Was there anything that if you could wave a magic wand and change what would that be?

# Chamber of Commerce

## "ARMED AND READY TO LEARN!"

# 89. Join The Chamber Of Commerce

Join your local Chamber of Commerce. Be an active member. Learn, teach, and connect with all local businesses. The more you give of your time and talent the more you will get back. There are networking opportunities that will help your business.

You will meet fellow store owners to share ideas on advertising, display, sales, merchandising, inventory, delivery and service. Your business will benefit from increased visibility and credibility. You will learn about new laws that will affect your business. You will have a voice in government through the Chamber of Commerce.

There are opportunities for free publicity and discounted advertising rates. Call your local Chamber of Commerce and join today!

# 90. Start A Charity

Start a charity that is near and dear to your heart. The benefits are literally endless. When you do something for others out of the goodness of your heart how do you feel about yourself? If you answered 'Great!', I would agree.

When you feel great about yourself how do you sell? If you answered great and I would again agree with you. How would you treat your employees? I think you get the point.

How does your customers feel about your store when they see you and your store promoting and contributing to your community? I would humbly submit to you that they feel great about you and your store.

My friend Jim Hicks who owns Mattress Mart in Zanesville is involved in numerous charities that raise his and his store's profile in the community. He has made a significant impact in Zanesville, Ohio. He is the President of the West Rangers Biddy League Football program. as well as contributes time, energy, and resources to Zanesville Charity Newsies, Fraternal Order of Police Zanesville, and is the FOP Associates President, Eagle Riders FOE 302.

I don't know how Jim does it all but he is one of my heroes. He gives so much to Zanesville that it doesn't surprise me that his store is supported by the community as well.

# 91. Earn Online Reviews

You may not like technology or embrace the internet but burying your head in the sand isn't going to make it go away. Either you earn and market 5 star online reviews or your store will be the victim of online reviews. Your store deserves the 5 star online reviews that it earns to be seen by the public.

You don't get 5 star online reviews, you earn them. Please re-read that. If your customers are not giving you 5 star online reviews you need to step back and start asking a lot of questions. The very first is, are you asking them? How are you asking them? When are you asking them? Are you helping your customers who are challenged by technology to give the 5 star review that your store has worked hard for?

Nothing that is good in life is easy. Does your sales process earn and ask for 5 star reviews? Your marketing must feature and model 5 star reviews. You must define for your customer the behaviors that ideal customers engage in. Those are giving testimonials, referrals, and 5 star online reviews as well as repeat purchases.

These behaviors should be seen by your prospect before they purchase. They should be used and modeled in your sales process and in all of your follow-up marketing after the sale and in your monthly newsletters.

When your machine is running well it produces an army of testimonials and 5 star online reviews that go to war everyday helping you win the battle for the customer's business! Is it a lot of work setting this up? Yes. Is it worth it? YES!

# 92. Be Like Joe!

Joe Girard that is. Who is Joe Girard? Guinness Book Of World Records recognizes Joe as the World's Greatest Salesmen. He did it in the automobile industry between 1963 and 1978. When you went Joe's office to write up a car you would see pictures of his customers with their new car and thank you notes written to Joe. Even though he won hundreds of awards they were not featured in his office where customers could see them.

All his customers could see is hundreds and thousands of pictures of happy customers with their new cars and Thank You notes. What was Joe communicating with his decor? My customer is the most important thing to me. You can be happy like my other customers too. What is your store communicating to your customers?

Knowing what your customer likes and doesn't like is the key to giving them an atmosphere that is interesting and engaging. Be like Joe! Show lots of happy customers enjoying your store's great products along with the Thank You Notes that your store has earned in your store will lead to more sales and more profits.

# 93. Your Store's Website

Your store's website is not a business card with hours and locations. It must engage your potential customer. You must offer something of value to the customer to get them to trade their contact information for your free report, book or video series. The bare minimum is their email address and name.

More advanced stores like Gardner's Mattress & More offer a second opt-in offer so they can get more complete contact information including the customer's address and phone number. They simply offer to mail a hard copy of their book to the customer in exchange for their address and phone number. Now they have complete contact information to market it to the customer with information instead of shouting "Hurry, Sale Ends Tomorrow!"

Ben McClure does a great job of engaging his customer's with a welcome video pointing the customer to their free book on how to avoid making mistakes while shopping for mattresses. Here is their website:

http://gardnersmattressandmore.com

See how the best marketers in the mattress industry do it! If a picture is worth a thousand words, what is a video worth?

# 94. Videos Sell!

Videos sell because they more fully engage our senses. When your customer reads print their eyes are engaged. When see a video their ears are now engaged as well. Some customers are visual learners and some are audio learners. Why not stack the deck? That's what using video is all about in your marketing.

One of the most effective uses of video is on a welcome page of a website. This entire book has been dedicated to differentiation of your store. The greatest differentiator is you! The store owner should warmly welcome their new potential customer to their website briefly state your mission and point them to your valuable free information that will serve as a lead capture for your marketing. Your opt-ins will dramatically increase by using video the way I described above. Do it now!

# 95. Newspapers Done Right!

Throughout this book I have encouraged you to do things differently than most other retail stores. Newspapers when done correctly can be very cost effective especially if you have multiple locations in an urban area or you have a strong local paper in a smaller town.

I could write a book just on this subject so forgive this short chapter on a very important subject. First off, just a broad overview most newspapers are dying. I am not saying don't use them. If you can get a positive enough return on your investment in newspaper advertising by all means use them. I say this because most newspapers will discount. Understand that published rates for newspaper ads are as real as rack rates for hotels. They are works of fiction. Never ever pay a regular published newspaper rate.

Newspapers that years ago were difficult to work with are now begging for business. For years I have coached my dealers to buy remnant color and insist upon guaranteed separation. Most newspapers in the past would resist giving my dealers guaranteed separation. The shoe is now on the other foot. Newspapers are now eager to do almost anything to capture your advertising dollars. Don't be too eager to sign a contract - some newspapers will let you have the contract rate as a trial without signing the contract.

If you are asking what guaranteed separation is, you are not alone. It simply means that if another direct competitor advertises in the paper they must place the ad on another page or the ad is free because they broke their contract with you. Not all papers have remnant color. But you need to ask if they have deals on remnant color. Remnant color is the crazy quilt of advertising. You don't get to pick the color but it's usually less than half of regular color. Sometimes it's less than a quarter of the normal price of color. If they offer remnant color you should take advantage of it. You lose a little creative control but the value is tremendous.

If you decide to advertise make sure your ad whenever possible is on the right hand side, called the reading page. Your ad will pull better if it's placed there. Also do everything possible to get above the fold. Including changing the shape of the ad to be tall and narrow to insure it gets above the fold. Those two tips together will create thousands of additional profit dollars for you. If that wasn't enough, here is my last tip worth hundreds of thousands of additional profit dollars for you. The most valuable real estate in your ad is the top left hand corner. Why? Because in America we are taught to read from left to right and from top to bottom. Make it count!

Got a story? Tell your local newspaper about it. You can get free publicity from the newspaper even if you don't advertise with them. But it helps a lot if you are a regular customer. Something that might be normal in your store might just be newsworthy. Gardner's Mattress & More received free publicity for their Dream Room in their local newspaper. How about work that your store is involved with for your charities? That should definitely be newsworthy. Remember when you negotiate with newspapers that you have the power not them. There are many successful stores who do not advertise in the newspaper. Never be emotionally attached to anything in your business. Never be attached to a type of media. Just because something is a great deal doesn't mean for your store that it will be a wise investment. Measure, evaluate, and then based on your store's results decide if a media will be used in the future including newspapers.

# 96. Brand Your Store

Have fun branding your store in new and creative ways. Here is a quick example at Gardner's Mattress & More customers can earn Ben Bucks that can be used to help purchase the items needed to complete a truly great sleep system like frames, sheets, pillows, protectors, and encasements.

The Ben Bucks actually have a picture of Ben McClure, co-owner of Gardner's Mattress & More and public figure for the store. It's a great way to further their store's brand. Find new and creative ways to brand your company.

Now for something more controversial. For sure a lot of manufactures will hate this advice. But a few smart retailers will love me for it. So here it is. Retailers create name brands. Name brands do not create successful retail stores. If you must use the name brand's POP but do not use the POP for your non brands.

I would only use my own branded POP for my store. I have no interest in building any brand for anyone. I can hear you now but "Pete, that would be so expensive! I don't need any more bills!" I hear you. Ask for a discount to use against purchases for the value of the "free POP" that you will not need anymore. That will probably cover more than half of the cost to brand your store and only your store with customized POP that helps you build your store's brand.

# 97. And The Winner Is!

There are local awards that you should spend some time and effort on to win. The Reader's Choice Awards are a good example for "Best Store To Buy A Mattress" Forgive me if I they call it something else now.

These awards might seem trivial to you and a bit contrived but for a mattress customer who hasn't bought in fifteen to twenty years it might make the difference between your store getting an opportunity to compete for the business.

Spend some time and thought into winning the awards in your area. Ask everyone you know to vote for your store and ask your customers to vote for your store in every conceivable way.

After you win it, feature it in every piece of marketing, branding, and feature it in your displays. Don't stop there. It needs to be in your sales process and in your email store signature. It needs to be on the back and sides of your delivery truck. It should be featured prominently in all letters and correspondence.

# 98. WOW!

There is never a bad time to wow a customer with an unexpected gift. One of the best times is on delivery. Use your imagination and pretend my example is real and ask yourself if this were me as a customer what would I think?

Ready? Imagine a nice clean truck pulls up to your house to deliver your new mattress system. Two uniformed smiling delivery men put out a red carpet leading to your home. They put booties on their feet and ask you a few questions and ask where the bed will be delivered to and then the walk through carefully planning their every move. They explain in detail sequentially what is going to happen.

They take care to be very careful of your house and even offer to vacuum under your bed with a hand held vacuum that they brought with them. After everything is installed they give you some final tips on how to take care of your new sleep system.

Then they give you an opportunity to rate your experience at the store they have a form for you to fill out and they are happy to wait while you fill it out. They also offer you to send it back if you are too busy to fill it out right then.

They leave a branded bag that includes branded pens and a paper note pad and two cake pops along with a few other items. They even delivered within a two hour window that they called you with a few hours prior to the deliver so you didn't have to wait around all day.

Are you thinking this is crazy? No retail store in their right mind could ever do all that. Here is a news flash for you this is what a Gardner's Mattress & More customer experiences everyday! Maybe you own a truly great store and you do many of these things but not all.

I am going to challenge you to try your best to duplicate this delivery experience the best you can. Who knows? maybe you can even add something to this to make it better? Maybe homemade brownies or cookies? I'm just spit balling.

Here is why delivery is so important - it is right here in this sacred space that all the promises made in your marketing and in your sales process are finally fulfilled. How your customer sees your store is largely determined by their delivery experience. Make sure it screams WE CARE!

Sending surprise gifts at special holidays or on your customer's birthday are great ways to keep the relationship going. At least do cards with a little handwritten note in it. I'm not asking you to give all your profit away but I am suggesting that you reinvest in your relationship with your customer so they are glad to give you testimonials, referrals, a 5 star online review, and repeat business.

# 99. Not Just Turkey!

At Thanksgiving you have a great opportunity to send Thanksgiving Day cards to your customers. When was the last time you received a Thanksgiving Day card from a business? Maybe never? If you received a few would it be safe to say there isn't a lot of competition for your customer's attention then?

Isn't Thanksgiving an appropriate holiday to say Thank You to your customers? I think so. Whenever possible write a personal note of thanks. That effort will be rewarded by your customer's loyalty. I have only done it once and it was a big hit with my dealers. It's now on my list to do it every year.

Always look for opportunities to have an impact on your customers when your competitors might be asleep at the wheel. Thanksgiving is a great example of catching your competitors napping when you can deliver a welcomed message of genuine thanks. Go for it!

# 100. Hire Studettes & Studs!

Salespeople are the Olympic athletes of the business world. You cannot create a superior customer experience with ordinary salespeople. Reread that. Let it sink in. I am sure throughout this book I have challenged you to think differently about your store.

I am really going to surprise you with this one so sit down and get ready to probably throw this book across the room. You will not like what I have to say but you need to hear it and implement this or take this book and throw it out and curse me.

Why do I need to hire studettes and studs? Nothing that is worthwhile in this life comes easy. If you are trying to be the best store it simply isn't possible to get there without truly great sales professionals. They are hard to come by and even harder to keep. You can do it if you do a few critical things. Are you ready?

First and foremost be picky. If something is bothering you in your gut just pass. It might mean you work a few more long weeks on the floor but that is preferable to hiring the wrong sales professional.

Here is where you throw the book out. You must become the best answer to a true retail sales professional's quest. What is their quest? To be respected, appreciated, and yes cared for to the point that they feel loved. You must give a lot to get a lot. There is no other way.

If you make a salesperson feel all those things they will never leave you. I am sure that you have been shocked and surprised in a bad way by many salespeople. You have to let that go and strive to have the best salespeople. A big part of being able to hire the best is your store's ability to deliver the best income producing opportunity available in the area with a great supportive and yes even loving work environment. Ask yourself, "what is the most I can pay for a great salesperson?" Are you still with me?

I didn't say it was going to be easy because it isn't. The only way you will ever liberate yourself to not be chained to your store is to hire, train, and retain a superior sales staff. There is no other way. The great Dan Kennedy always talks about working on your business not in it.

When you have the best sales professionals you will be able to get some time away from the store so you can have the space and perspective to really work on your business instead of getting drawn into every bit of drama that humans create. I literally could write an entire book just on this subject but we must move on to our last chapter.

THANK YOU!

# 101. The Single Biggest Mistake Stores Make & How To Correct It!

Congratulations on making it through 100 short chapters! I have thrown a lot of ideas at you in this book. I wrestled with putting this chapter first or last in the book. Why? Because it is the most important chapter in the book.

I have been blessed to have met and worked with hundreds of stores throughout this country over the past thirty three years. The single biggest mistake that I consistently see is stores that needlessly give their profits away by simply not charging enough for their products.

The simple fix for this problem is to raise your prices. You might need to drop some lines and add others to achieve this. It won't happen overnight but chances are you should raise your prices.

If you look at business history if you choose to be the low price store you will end up out of business sooner or later. It isn't a sustainable position. Am I saying Wal-Mart will one day be out of business? Yes. Absolutely they will if they don't extract themselves from the lowest priced store position.

Throughout this book you probably thought, "Pete, that's a great idea but where is the money going to come from?" My answer to you is if you are 100% happy with your store don't change a thing. You probably bought this book and invested your time in reading it because you want to improve your store. The money to pay for these recommended improvements will come from raising your prices.

There is no free lunch. You cannot offer great service with really low prices. Those two things are mutually exclusive. There are many different ways to retail furniture and mattresses. There are warehouse models. There are shopping experience models. There are high end, low end, and everything in between. They are all valid.

This book has focused on creating a furniture or mattress store that is a middle to higher end store that focuses on delivering a superior customer experience. It also when followed to its successful implementation creates a business that allows more security and freedom for the business owner.

Thank you for investing your time, energy, and money into the ideas presented in this book. Visit my website at www.peteprimeau.com for more sales tips and business building tips. Please let me know how this book has benefited you and your store by emailing me at peteprimeau@ameritech.net.

Sell a million today!

Pete Primeau

P.S. I thought I would end this book on an uplifting reminder of what it means to be an entrepreneur. I did not write this and it comes from a gentleman named Jack Miller. Jack was in the real estate business and is no longer with us, but his thoughts of gratitude are a great reminder for all of us. As you read each, consider your own life and reflect on all that you have to be thankful for.

# What I am Thankful For

by Jack Miller

*I am healthy, productive and happy.*

*I'm surrounded by family and friends who support what I do.*

*I live and work in a lovely place that I selected myself.*

*I don't have to commute to work at all. No rush-hour traffic.*

*I get to wear (or not wear) anything I like all day long.*

*My pay is based solely on how long and productively I want to work.*

*I get to start work as early as I want, and to work as late as I want.*

*I can take vacations where and when I want without asking permission.*

*I have no boss to make me waste my time and do stupid things.*

*I get to make all the decisions regarding my financial security and that of my family.*

*I am free to take responsibility for all my activities, good and bad.*

*I can do what I do in any place in America and in many foreign lands.*

*I am able to make more than most of the people in the world.*

*Because I work for myself, my company won't be merged.*

*I don't have to worry about being laid off, down sized or fired.*

*My retirement plan is within my control.*

# Bonus Chapters

As a thank you to you for investing your time, energy, and money in this book! I wanted to give you something extra. These articles are great to incorporate into your sales training. I hope you enjoy them and profit through their message and implementation.

# The New Rules for Selling Furniture & Mattresses

It was 1982 and I was still in college. I started selling furniture. I had to call credit cards into a call center and wait for an operator to give me an authorization code. Then I would manually run the credit card through a machine with multiple copies utilizing carbon paper. If you were not careful you would get black ink all over your hands. The transaction took an average of 5 minutes, but could take up to 20 minutes. Today the same transaction is done in less than a minute.

Finance deals took 2-3 working days for approval. Today the same transaction is concluded in a max of thirty minutes. If the consumer's credit is good it is approved in minutes.

The most expensive sofa on the floor was $999. No one ever bought it. There were very few if any real leather sofas available. Today you can buy genuine leather for $999. The most expensive mattress set was $999. Our best selling queen set was priced at $399. If I sold a $599 set, high fives were in order. Today the average is $799. Today there are queen mattress sets that sell for $5,000 to $7,000 in mid priced stores.

There have been many changes. These are just a few. Please go to www.peteprimeau.com and add a comment with the changes you have noticed along with your new rule for selling furniture and mattresses. Here are the top responses from the question, "What changes have you seen in our industry in the past twenty years?" The poll includes furniture and mattress stores in Ohio & Western Pennsylvania. I look forward to your feedback.

**The Internet-** Customers now use the internet to educate themselves prior to shopping in the store. There is good information on the Internet and there is also bad information on the Internet. You need to know both. You face the only new objection in sales in the past 100 years. It is "I can find it cheaper on the Internet." The new rule is to do Internet research everyday so you know what information your customer is accessing. If a consumer makes this statement to you and it is possible for you to get on the Internet, this objection can be handled easily with your manager's assistance.

**Instant Gratification-** Once the customer decides on a product they want it now or sooner. This is also known as the McDonald's mentality. Customers are conditioned to immediate gratification for a number of reasons. Many work two jobs and between the responsibilities of home and work have very little time. The common complaint is that my life is speeding by. They want answers and product now. They do not have the time to invest in things that do not add quality to their lives. Be light on your feet. Know your product. Practice being a good problem solver. Serve you customers' needs. Diffuse the objection early, how soon do you need the ___, when do you plan on completing your room or project?

As a salesperson you do not have control over the inventory. However there are two new rules that will help you make more sales. The new rule is to know what inventory you have on hand that is available to ship right away. If you know the approximate delivery times for arriving merchandise your customer will appreciate your attentiveness with their loyalty. The other new rule is to qualify the customer on their delivery needs **prior** to presenting product.

**The Economy-** News Flash! It is better this year than last year! It is not fantastic yet but most of my dealers are up this year. The basics never change whether the economy is good or bad. The new rule is pay attention to every aspect of your sales business. This includes your education as a salesperson. When was the last time you read a book about selling or went to a seminar?

**Bigger Furniture-** Today there are more oversized sofas and bedroom sets than ever before. While many customers enjoy these new larger luxury items, some customers get their hopes dashed when the item will not fit into their home. Professional salespeople avoid this situation by anticipating it and dealing with it proactively with good questions. The new rule is to thoroughly explore the customer's needs who are considering oversized furniture. Successful retail salespeople help their customers avoid the unpleasant task of having to re-select because an item did not fit.

**Ultra Premium Mattresses-** Mattresses have more than doubled in price and comfort. Everyone in our industry should say thank you to Tempur-Pedic. They have raised the selling price for the entire industry. The new rule is let the customer experience the best mattress in the store in a non threatening way. Ask the customer for their opinion. "Mrs. Jones please try this bed and tell me if you think it's comfortable." Please resist the urge to give any product information until Mrs. Jones gives you a reaction to the bed. Have fun with creatively showing the best bed in a non threatening way. Some of these rules are not new at all.

# Show Me The Money

When I recently asked you what articles about selling you would like to read, the most popular response was "Show me how to make more money." I cannot thoroughly answer that in one article but I can share several ideas that will help you immediately.

**Money is a by product of Serving.** Want to make more money? The top salespeople focus on serving their customers. The money they make is simply the result of serving the needs and wants of their customers.

**Top Salespeople are in business for themselves.** They create their own traffic. They network and prospect continuously to increase the number of customers they see everyday.

**They Prepare.** They know their products, inventory, advertising, finance offers, policies and procedures, and those of their competitors. I must acknowledge John F. Lawhon's breakthrough book here "Selling Retail".

**They Shop their Competition.** You must shop your competitors or have them shopped. Failure to do this will lead to missed sales.

**They Educate Themselves.** They embrace new ideas. One top salesperson shared that his favorite sales trainers were Dale Carnegie and Tom Hopkins. Not only did he buy the books he invested in their seminars! He saw Hopkins twice! He did not wait for his company to train him. He invested in his own business. His sales business! Among my favorite authors/speakers are Zig Zigler, Tom Hopkins, Brian Tracy, and the fabulous Jeffrey Gitomer. A big Thank You to Jonathan DiPrinzio for turning me on to Jeffrey Gitomer. After twenty nine years of success in selling, I am still learning.

**Continuous Improvement.** Top Salespeople seek to learn every day in every way. They study their coworkers for new ideas and techniques. They become friends with the sales representatives so they can learn everything they can from them.

**They Measure their Success.** They know their metrics. They measure their closing rates and their average ticket. They strive to improve their statistics. They are on a mission to improve their service to their customers. They know that to achieve true success everyone must win.

**They Follow-up.** Before I read John F. Lawhon's "Selling Retail" I would send thank you notes only to customers that bought from me. After I read the book I started sending thank you notes to all my customers. Lawhon explained that one of the differences between good and great salespeople was the great ones sent thank you notes to all their customers. He was right! My income went up. The most important follow-up is a phone call the day after a customer shops your store.

**Find a Mentor.** Who do you know that is the best? Model yourself after them, but do not lose yourself. Follow the principles of your mentor's success but be yourself. On my YouTube channel you can see the video I created about me and my mentor. Just go to http://www.peteprimeau.com/book-links.

# Selling Furniture & Mattresses – I'm Hired, Now What?

In the past day I received two emails from two different new salespeople thanking me for their initial mattress training. They then asked me what they could do to be as productive as fast as possible. My answers included both short term and long term strategies and tactics. Here they are!

**Mentor–** Model yourself after a successful salesperson. Find someone to help guide you (hopefully more than one).

**Perspective-** Never forget the first time you shopped for mattresses. If you remember the emotions and thoughts you felt then you will have empathy for your customer. That empathy will help you to engage your customer in a meaningful way that will uncover their desired outcomes which is the first step in any selling process.

**Basic Knowledge-** Learning the terminology for mattresses is a great place to start. Also learning the sizes is imperative. The Better Sleep Council is a great source for unbiased non brand specific information. Your customers use it and you should too. You can access it from here: http://www.peteprimeau.com/book-links.

**The Three Little Bears-** "This one is too firm. This one is too soft. This one is just right!" Lay down on every mattress in your store and catalogue them in your mind from the softest to the firmest making special notes which mattresses have similar feels. Knowing how the mattresses feel in relation to each other is critical foundational knowledge for any salesperson. It enables you to direct the customer based on the feedback they give you.

**Eliminate Confusion-** One of the challenges we have when working with a retail customer is to narrow the selection based on good questions, comfort tests, and feedback from them. The easiest system is comfort selling. To read more, visit: http://www.peteprimeau.com/book-links.

**Commitment-** Top retail salespeople all have one thing in common. They are committed to their success. They view themselves as the president of their own sales company. To read more, visit:

http://www.peteprimeau.com/book-links.

**Shop Your Competitors-** When a salesperson is new they should take advantage of their anonymity and shop their competitors before they get shopped. Shopping your competitors provides you with a wealth of information that will help you make more sales.

# It's Your Sales Business!

All great retail salespeople have one thing in common. They view their sales as their own business. This mindset allows them to make significantly more money than their peers. More importantly these top producers are happy and usually enjoy great relationships in all aspects of their lives. Here's what they do.

**Early-** They are usually the first into the store and the last to leave. Why? Because, they work for "themselves", they are willing to pay the price for success in full and in advance.

**Commitment-** They are committed to success. They do things that other people are unwilling to do to achieve their goals. They go the extra mile to serve their customers and are rewarded with their loyalty.

**Integrity-** Top producers always tell the truth. Their word is their bond. Their customers trust them and always ask for them.

**Invest-** Top salespeople invest in their business. They buy sales books. They go to sales seminars. If their company does not supply Thank You cards, they buy their own. They are constantly looking for an edge to serve their customers better. They invest 3% of their earnings back into their sales business.

**Educate-** They constantly want to learn. One of the most interesting observations I've made in the past twenty nine years is that top salespeople study other salespeople and try to learn from them as well as from their reps. They use their downtime productively to improve their selling skills.

**Create-** Top salespeople create their own traffic. They cultivate an army of loyal customers who only buy from them. They are constantly prospecting for customers. They do not wait for door traffic. They talk to their neighbors or anyone that will listen about the store they work at. They promote their sales business.

**Execute**– They follow-up on their sales in every way. They always make sure everything is OK with their customers. You know you are on the right track when you are occasionally accused of being paranoid. In addition to sending a written Thank You notes, they follow-up with a phone call to make sure the customer is happy with their purchase. They also start the buying cycle for the next item by offering to keep their eyes open for the next purchase. Evaluate your sales business and consider it your own. What can you do to create more traffic for your business?

Visit my site at:

www.PetePrimeau.com for my podcasts, articles and more!

# Primeau Furniture Sales Team

Jenny Primeau- Jenny is the VP of Primeau Furniture Sales. Jenny has been an accountant her entire life. She does whatever it takes to keep our customers happy. If we gave out an MVP award at Primeau Furniture Sales She would win it every year!!

Nick Markos- Senior Partner at Primeau Furniture Sales. Nick is 24 year veteran of the home furnishing's industry. Nick increases his dealers business by improving their advertising, display, merchandising, sales training, and service. Years ago several of my dealers implored me to bring Nick into our business. Bringing Nick onboard as a partner is one of my best business decisions ever!

Wayne Baker- Wayne is a 36 year veteran of the home furnishing's industry. He works with dealers in Southern Ohio, West Virginia, and Kentucky. He is a traditional rep who is so capable that he creates all the advertising and all the sales training at many of his dealer's stores. Wayne hang glides, scuba dives, and flies airplanes in his spare time. He also plays the guitar, piano, violin, fiddle, and harmonica.

Made in the USA
Monee, IL
30 September 2023